To Joe,

With every

best wish

+ God's blessing,

Michael Seed

1994

I WILL SEE YOU IN
HEAVEN

I WILL SEE YOU IN

HEAVEN

where animals don't bite...

EDITED BY
MICHAEL SEED

St Paul Publications

Illustrations by Annie Tempest

Designed by Chapter & Verso

St Paul Publications
Middlegreen, Slough SL3 6BT, United Kingdom

Copyright © St Paul Publications 1991
ISBN 085439 381 1
Printed by Dotesios Ltd, Trowbridge, Wiltshire

St Paul Publications is an activity of the priests and brothers of the
Society of St Paul who proclaim the Gospel through the media of social
communication

In my dream I visited heaven
and hell.
'Are you hungry?' St Peter asked.
'Yes,' I replied.

In two separate rooms
a banquet was in progress.
Each guest
had just one long spoon
to eat with.

In the first hall
they were trying to feed themselves
which was plain impossible.
For the long spoons
hindered rather than helped.
And they were angry,
frustrated,
miserable.
'This is hell,'
St Peter explained.

In the other hall
the guests fed one another.
And they were happy.
Then smiling,
St Peter turned to me and said,
'This is heaven!'

Anonymous

Contributors

ALDINUCCI, Abbot Vittorino

ALTON, David

ANTHONY OF SOUROZH, Metropolitan

ARCHER, Jeffrey

BEST, Keith

BLINKKLU, Amaro

BONO OF 'U2'

BURROWS, General Eva

BUSH, Kate

CAREY, Archbishop George

CARTLAND, Dame Barbara

CASSIDY, Cardinal Edward

CASTRO, Rev Prof. Emilio

CHESHIRE, Lord

CHOMET, Seweryn

CHURCHILL-COLEMAN, Commander

DALAI LAMA, His Holiness the

DE CUELLAR, Javier Pérez

FILOCHOWSKI, Julian

FULBRIGHT, Senator J. William

FURNESS, Lord

GASCOIGNE, Paul

GIELGUD, Sir John

GRAHAM, Dr Billy

GREENE, Graham

GREGORIOS, Metropolitan

HAILSHAM, Lord

HANRATTY, Dr J.F.

HARGREAVES, Ken

HRH THE PRINCESS ANNE

HRH THE DUCHESS OF KENT

HSH RAINIER III, Prince of Monaco

HUME, Cardinal George Basil

JAKOBOVITS, Lord

JOSEPH, Jenny

KENT, Bruce

LEONARD, Bishop Graham

LONGFORD, Lord

MAJOR, John

MARTIN, J.L.

MARTIN, Thomas

MEHTA, Cyrus P.

MENUHIN, Sir Yehudi

MILLIGAN, Spike

MOORE, Dudley

MUIR, Frank

NEWTON, John

PATTEN, Christopher

RATZINGER, Cardinal Joseph

RAYBOULD, Major Brian

RICHARD, Cliff

ROSSI, Marie-Louise

RUNCIE, Lord Robert

SHENOUDA III, His Holiness

SKINNER, Dennis

SMOKER, Barbara

SOPER, Lord

STERNBERG, Sir Sigmund

SULZBERGER, Arthur Ochs

SUTHERLAND, Dame Joan

TAIZÉ, Brother Roger of

TAYLOR, Rev Michael

TEMPEST, Annie

TEMPLETON, Sir John M.

TERESA, Mother

TUTU, Archbishop Desmond

VAFADARI, Shahrokh R.

WEATHERILL, Bernard

WEST, Morris

WIDDECOMBE, Ann

WILLEBRANDS, Cardinal J.G.M.

WILLIAMSON, Malcolm

WILLIS, Norman

WILSON, Lord

WILSON, Lady Mary

WOGAN, Terry

To
Mother Teresa of Calcutta

Acknowledgements

I am indebted to such a vast number of people that I have to start by apologising to those who are not mentioned here.

Firstly, my thoughts go to my grandmother, parents and family with God ('I will see you in heaven') and to Bishop William Gordon Wheeler.

Very special thanks are due to all the contributors who, despite their busy schedules, were so generous with their time and cherished thoughts.

I also thank Peter Hannigan and the boys of Westminster Cathedral Choir School; Mrs Barbier and the children of Burdett-Coutts Primary School; Mrs Weller and the children of St Vincent de Paul Nursery and Primary School; Sister Elizabeth, DC, and the girls of Blackbrook House Community School; Jane Eizenhauer and St Joseph's Hospice, Hackney; Major Brian Raybould, staff and residents of the Salvation Army Hostel, Westminster; Michael for 'Footprints'; 'Christhouse', Washington, DC; Father Padraig Regan, CM, and the Passage Day Centre for the Homeless; the Ecumenical Society of the Blessed Virgin Mary; Annie Tempest, the greatest cartoonist in the world, who continued with heavenly thoughts after she had broken her leg; Mark Twomey and Steven Grieve without whose time and energy this book would not have taken shape; Janet Tempest and the co-workers of Mother Teresa for their warm support; the Community of Franciscan Friars of the Atonement to whom I owe everything; Joan Bond and Friars Gerard and Alexander of the Catholic Central Library my colleagues at Westminster Cathedral; and Cardinal Basil Hume, who accused me of stealing other people's thoughts – forgive me!

And finally I wish to acknowledge my indebtedness to the following for permission to use copyright material:

Vintage Books, New York: *Heaven – A History* by C. McDannell and B. Lang; Ateliers et Presses de Taizé for the Prayer of Brother Roger; the Francis Thompson Society: *The Hound of Heaven* by Francis Thompson; Penguin Books: *Selected Poems* by Rabindranath Tagore; Church Pastoral Aid Society: *The Singer* by Calvin Miller; The Bodley Head: *Be Not Afraid* by Andre Frossard in conversation with Pope John Paul II; Fathers of the Church Inc., New York: St John Chrysostom in *Fathers of the Church*; Michael Joseph: *A Book of Peace* by Elizabeth Goudge; The Daughters of St Paul, Boston: *The Message of John Paul I;* Carlin Music Corporation: *Day by Day* from the musical *Godspel* by Stephen Schwartz and J.M. Tebelak and *The Impossible Dream* from the musical *Man of La Mancha* by Mitchell Leigh and

Joseph Darton; The Church Union: *The Gospel is for Everyone* by Dr Graham Leonard; Campania Financiera Perlina: *The Heretic* by Morris West; Darton, Longman & Todd: *They Speak by Silences* by a Carthusian monk and *Living Prayer* by Metropolitan Anthony of Sourozh; SCM Press: *Jewish Prayer and Worship* by W.W. Simpson; Gerald Duckworth & Co: *Sonnets and Verse* by Hilaire Belloc; The Ecumenical Society of the Blessed Virgin Mary: *An Ecumenical Office of Mary the Mother of Jesus;* Faber & Faber: *Warning* by Jenny Joseph in *The Faber Book of 20th Century Women's Poems and Plays* and *The Poetical Works of Rupert Brooke* edited by G. Keynes; Weidenfeld & Nicholson and Wheel Shore Ltd: *On Acting* by Lord Laurence Olivier; Leda Productions Inc: *As Time Goes By* by Laurence Leamer; Kate Bush Music Ltd and EMI Music Publishing Ltd: 'Sat in Your Lap' from the album *The Dreaming* by Kate Bush; Christ House, Washington, DC: *The Family at Christ House* edited by D. Husby; Franciscan Herald Press: *Franciscan Readings;* Burns & Oates: *Butler's Lives of the Saints;* Collins: *Mister God, This Is Anna* by Fynn, *An Impossible God* by Frank Topping and *Something Beautiful for God* by Malcolm Muggeridge; Tavistock Publications: *On Death and Dying* by Elisabeth Kübler-Ross; Harper & Row, New York: *A Letter of Consolation* by Henri Nouwen; Hutchinson Books: *New Poems* by Lady Mary Wilson; William Heinemann: *The Power and the Glory* by Graham Greene; Catholic University of America Press: *Eschatology: Death and Eternal Life* by Cardinal Joseph Ratzinger; Hierarchy of England and Wales Liturgy Office: extracts from the *Divine Office;* St Paul Publications: *Where's God in All This?* by Leonard Cheshire and *To Be A Pilgrim* by Cardinal George Basil Hume; Warner Chappell and Blue Mountain Music for the quote by Bono from the song *I Still Haven't Found What I'm Looking For.*

Every effort has been made to trace copyright holders. My apologies for any omissions, which will be rectified in subsequent editions.

Michael Seed

Foreword

We all long for heaven where God is, but we have it in our power to be in heaven with him right now. To be happy with him now means loving as he loves, giving as he gives, serving as he serves, rescuing as he rescues, touching him in the distressing disguise of the poorest of the poor by being his presence, his love, his compassion in their lives.

Let us pray for each other that we may be the sunshine of God's love – the hope of eternal happiness to all whose lives we touch daily.

Heaven for me will be the joy of being with Jesus and Mary and all the other saints and angels, and all our poor – all of us going home to God.

Let us ask Jesus and Mary, the saints and angels to pray for us that we do God's work with love and that we do not spoil it – the beauty of God's work.

Father Michael has compiled this book and I am sure it will do great good to the glory of God and peace in the world. Keep the joy of loving God in your heart and share this joy with all you meet. Let us pray. God bless you.

Mother Teresa MC

Welcome to the World of Heaven

Easter Sunday afternoon 1985, that 'heavenly' time after Sunday lunch. The television was turned on but not much attention was given. I was relaxing with friends, drinking coffee. Suddenly people were looking at the telly and there was silence. A little boy of six was talking from Helen House, a hospice for children in Oxford. Garvan, who was in fact twelve years old, had a rare bone marrow disease. The tears stood in our eyes as we listened to the words of this little boy, who would be dead within six weeks:

> *Dying is not really dying, it is just like opening an old door into a new room which is heaven... there you will meet the people you knew on earth and I am looking forward to that.*

Garvan was trying to comfort his parents with these words. He asked them not to worry about him and told them that he would always love them.

Many such sacred moments are presented in this book, from the time of our birth till the moment of our death. Our life on this earth is very short. Every breath taken is precious. It is a gift from God our Mother and Father. You have taken a leap into heaven on earth.

The 'shock' of heaven is here! We may be 'waiting' for heaven, but heaven is already here. Perhaps we are 'out' while God is always 'in'! God is in when we are angry or upset, when we have lost a loved one, when we are happy and there is no one to share our joy.

All this may sound very well indeed – but what about our doubts? How can I say 'Our Father who art in heaven' when I need him here on earth? On a very quiet Saturday morning – a morning when I needed God so very badly – there was a knock on the door of our house. I heard the voice of a lady, 'Come quickly, I think it is Lillian, she is dead...' It was the body of my mother. She had taken her life. My father and grandfather rushed out. I remained in the house with my grandmother. I was eight years old then. Within two years my father and grandfather would also be dead. So I was raised by a loving grandmother. She said her prayers every morning and night. Like the little boy Garvan, she never doubted the care of her God. My first prayer I learned from that great lady (now with God also) with the words: 'I will see you in heaven.' That is my prayer for you.

Faith is a gift from God. It is often a most painful gift but where God is, there is no fear. Never be afraid of your doubts – the tunnel of life can often be very dark, but there always is light, if we would only see.

Heaven is peace when there is war in our lives. Heaven is the most insignificant action done out of love for another. Heaven is the basis of all love; it is our very hope and light. Heaven is the young Mary, fearful at the invitation from the angel to be the mother of God. Heaven is our death and the death of all whom we love. Heaven is that state where I find union with God.

I have compiled this book as a Christian or at least as one who tries to live up to that title. Nonetheless, I have drawn upon sources from other great religious traditions as well as from secular thinking. There are also contributions from children, the dying, the needy, those living in night-shelters and many others.

I pray that these pages may stir in you a longing for God and an irrepressible love of neighbour, bringing earth a little nearer to heaven!

Michael Seed

8 September 1991

HEAVEN

on earth...

1O DOWNING STREET
LONDON SW1A 2AA

THE PRIME MINISTER

4 February 1991

Dear Father Seed,

THOUGHTS ON HEAVEN

Thank you for your letter inviting me to contribute to your
anthology on Heaven. There is much of what I conceive of as
Heaven in the poem "The Kingdom of God" by Francis
Thompson.

I hope that this is suitable.

Yours sincerely,

John Major

The Kingdom of God
'In no Strange Land'

O world invisible, we view thee,
O world intangible, we touch thee,
O world unknowable, we know thee,
Inapprehensible, we clutch thee!

      Does the fish soar to find the ocean,
      The eagle plunge to find the air –
      That we ask of the stars in motion
      If they have rumour of thee there?

Not where the wheeling systems darken,
And our benumbed conceiving soars! –
The drift of pinions, would we hearken,
Beats at our own clay-shuttered doors.

      The angels keep their ancient places; –
      Turn but a stone, and start a wing!
      'Tis ye, 'tis your estrangéd faces,
      That miss the many-splendoured thing.

But (when so sad thou canst not sadder)
Cry; – and upon thy so sore loss
Shall shine the traffic of Jacob's ladder
Pitched betwixt Heaven and Charing Cross.

      Yea, in the night, my Soul, my daughter,
      Cry – clinging Heaven by the hems;
      And lo, Christ walking on the water
      Not of Gennesareth, but Thames!

Francis Thompson

What if Earth
Be but the shadow of Heaven, and things therein
Each to other like, more than on Earth is thought?

John Milton, *Paradise Lost*

Heaven

Dear friends. Beauty in house and garden. The changing of the Seasons. Music, especially Bach, Mozart, Purcell, Chopin. Fellowship in work, colleagues old and new. Vivid memories thankfully stored up. Hopes continuing. Animal devotion.

Hell

Miseries of the world — wars, disease, starvation, poverty. Desolating outlook. Sickness and death of loved friends. Fear of illness and loss of memory. Inability to communicate. Diminution of faculties. Misgivings and reluctance to tackle new problems and increasing distrust of ability to enjoy more than a few people at a time. Shame at self-centredness and past mistakes and sins never forgotten.

Paradise

Wonderful parents and upbringing.
The marvels of great literature, especially Shakespeare. A long career in the profession I chose and the inestimable blessing of having worked with great artists and travelled in so many parts of the world engaged in projects that brought me so much fascination and discovery over so many years.

Sir John Gielgud

We study heaven because it reflects a deep and profound longing in Christianity to move beyond this life and to experience more fully the divine. The ways in which people imagine heaven tell us how they understand themselves, their families, their society, and their God. They give us insight into both the private and public dimensions of Western culture. Changing ideas about love, friendship, work, God, and spiritual growth in the other life can serve as guide-lines for understanding cultural ideas and ideals of this life. Heaven is not merely a collection of idle fantasies, a projection of human hopes, or a reflection of religious doctrine. We would go a step beyond Ludwig Feuerbach's admission that heaven is the key to the deepest mysteries of religion and venture that heaven can be used as a key to our Western culture.

C. McDannel & B. Lang, *Heaven – A History*

I once read a two volume work entitled *The Faith of a Moralist* by A. Taylor. I really remember little of what I read except a fascinating and indeed compelling image of heaven and it was this.

The author said in heaven we will have no time for jealousy because we will all be so engrossed in the beauty that is God, discovering ever new levels of beauty in God who is the Infinite One. And like lovers or those who have discovered something beautiful, we would want others to share in the beauty, the loveliness, the holiness that we had seen and they in their turn would be eager to share with us what they had so ecstatically found.

There would thus be this discovery and eagerness to share forever and ever, because God is an infinity of beauty, goodness and love – a love that I believe would ultimately be compellingly irresistible.

I wonder what we would do if we discovered a Hitler or an Amin in heaven – they having found God's love quite irresistible?

Archbishop Desmond Tutu

Looking back over a very long life I am astonished at the comparative indifference of my earlier years to the prospect of life after death. I professed it publicly as a Methodist preacher. I remember that I recited it regularly in my prayers – but like so many human issues it seemed such a long way off that for me it was relatively unimportant.

Now I am an old man, and to put it simply, death is a very 'live' issue and words like heaven and hell have an unavoidable immediacy. In fact I am now convinced that to realize that our human experience on this planet is not the sum total of reality has become an absolute requirement. Unless there is something beyond this earthly realm, 'sound and fury signifying nothing' loom as almost a final verdict on human experience.

All our aspirations as to the quality of life after death, all its anticipations of human relationships restored after being severed on earth, all questions about what it will be like for the good, and what it presages for the bad and, above all, will I be happy and fulfilled, or disappointed – all this ultimately depends on whether heaven is a 'must or a myth'.

I am now satisfied that if there is any truth anywhere, it can only be credible if there is an optimistic future beyond the grave.

To believe and to assert that 'God is love' demands a realm of existence where fulfilment of his loving purpose can happen – and it cannot fully happen in the world of time and space and matter. We can and ought to begin the pilgrimage, here and now, to his Kingdom, but we need that eternal world so that those who start out, like Christian in *Pilgrim's Progress*, can not only find the wages of going on from day to day, but can catch the sound of the trumpets that sound for them on the other side.

The Rev Lord Soper
Former President of the Methodist Conference

Jesus the Christ,
it is because your forgiveness
radiates trust
that peace of heart is possible
and even certain.
Through your Holy Spirit,
you are living within us all
and this,
already on this earth,
with you the Risen One,
is the beginning of eternity,
of a life that will never end.

Brother Roger
Founder of the Ecumenical
Community at Taizé, France

Child: Do you believe that a missionary goes to heaven and a cannibal goes to the other place?

Father: Of course!

Child: What happens when the missionary is inside the cannibal?

The lamp of earth burns in the lap of Mother Earth.
The evening star looks down upon her wistfully,
    to watch her light.
That light is like the anxious look of the beloved, lost to itself;
    it flickers like a fear that throbs within a mother's heart.
That light burns within the heart of the green earth,
    and trembles with pain in the restless wind.
The voice of the evening star descends from the skies, bringing benediction,
    and the immortal flame is a thirst to burn up in a mortal flame.

Rabindranath Tagore, *Lipika*

I think heaven is a place of happiness,
where dreams can come true.
Heaven is a place where there is no pain and
no one will age.

People will be able to speak to each other,
no matter what language they speak
An animal would understand English as well
as being able to talk in English.
Anyone who goes there can play with his toys
as he did on earth. Only one difference will
occur while he is playing and that is
cuddly-toys and carved figures will come to life.
You will not need to pay for anything and
the weather will always be good.

Alexander, aged 9
A chorister of Westminster Cathedral Choir School

My heaven is an interior landscape – not subject to anyone else's frame of reference. It is an eternal now – non-dynamic, non-entropic. Although my heaven will be unique, within I will feel spiritually connected like a single perfect stitch in God's huge tapestry that was, in earthly life, just a lost piece of colourful wool waiting to be threaded and included. In this interior landscape I would be suspended in a state of total fulfilment and peace. My five senses would be active within the eternal now:

Sight: A beautiful meadow, with wild flowers, lavender, trees, hills and a stream. Early morning sunlight.

Sound: The trickling of the stream over stones.

Smell: Lavender and new grass.

Touch: Warm earth.

Taste: Fresh garden mint.

Annie Tempest
Cartoonist of the *Daily Mail* and the 1990 Strip-Cartoonist of the Year

I have a problem. I would like to believe in heaven and an afterlife but I can find no evidence of it. There is much spoken about the afterlife and the glories that it contains but personally I cannot feel that such a place exists; that does not stop me living a life of a good Christian whose philosophy, through the teachings of Jesus Christ, I try to observe closely mixed with a touch of Buddhism on the environmental side.

Shall I put it this way: I find heaven is on earth, I am stunned by the beauty of a blade of grass, can I say more.

If there is a heaven then I will consider it a bonus.

Spike Milligan
Actor and author

Each of us can create here and now our own heaven or hell. The one thing over which we have most control is our own mind.

We can choose to focus on the seven deadly sins which are Pride, Lust, Sloth, Envy, Anger, Covetousness and Gluttony, which are hellish. Or we can focus our minds on the heavenly fruit of the Spirit, which are Love, Joy, Peace, Patience, Kindness, Goodness, Faithfulness, Gentleness and Self-control.

Sir John M. Templeton

As I don't believe in God, it is hard for me to believe in heaven... except as we know it on this earth! I suppose I would like to stress the immediacy of heaven, since I'm not a believer... so what other choice do I have! It seems almost that one can have an even more startlingly vivid notion of heaven, if one is a non-believer... because we do know (quite certainly) this is all we have!

Dudley Moore

A sense of well being, of peace with the world and humanity steals over you the minute you set foot in your boat. You are the master and can forget your work and the troubles of the world. You become a part of your ship, graceful as a bird, skimming effortlessly over the waves, testing your skill, not against anyone else's but against nature, your ideals and the person you would like to be.

Sailing on a sunny day, with a fresh breeze blowing, with maybe somebody you really care for, is the nearest thing to heaven I will ever get on this earth.

HRH The Princess Anne, The Princess Royal

I desire for you all… that in spirit and heart you will strive and endeavour until the world of war become the world of peace; the world of darkness the world of light; satanic conduct be turned into heavenly behaviour; the ruined places become built up; the sword be turned into the olive branch; the flash of hatred become the flame of the love of God and the noise of the gun the voice of the Kingdom; the soldiers of death the soldiers of life; all the nations of the world one nation; all races as one race; and all national anthems harmonized into one melody. Then this material realm will be paradise, the earth heaven.

Tablets of 'Abdu'l-Bahá

It is said that a monk was invited by a famous rich man. The host and his family were devout Christians who were accustomed to the devotion of inviting holy people: monks, bishops, priests, deacons and other church dignitaries to their house to feed them and receive their blessings. The man wished to learn more about the Holy Orthodox Faith. The host, taking this very pious monk to his house, shewed him an imposing mansion. Furthermore, he shewed him the chapel with the holy ikons which were in the house.

The host then asked the monk to tell him about heaven, God and salvation. He was particularly interested about how he could go to heaven, and what type of place it was. The monk became very serious. After a pause for deep thought, the monk told his host, 'Thank you for inviting me into your very large house, but I wonder if you have thought of a very small place in heaven rather than a mansion. You must consider and take care of mansions on earth, but for a mansion in heaven...?'

Metropolitan Gregorios
Greek Orthodox Archbishop of Thyateria and Great Britain

Jesus informed his followers he would make for them a mansion in his Father's house.

One of the modern translations changes the word mansion to home, which for me takes on a new meaning.

In this age a man can have a mansion which is certainly not a home. For me a home is where families unite, love and share each other's company, where everyone is happy and content. A man can have a mansion and not be happy; but to have a true home is happiness. It could be a flat, house, caravan or mansion, but only if it's 'home' is it worthwhile.

Jesus promises his followers a home in heaven, and this song from the *Salvation Army Song Book* describes it admirably:

> I have a home that is fairer than day,
> And my dear Saviour has shown me
> The Way.
> Oft when I'm sad, and temptations arise
> I look to my home in the skies.
>
> Friends I shall see who have journed before,
> And landed safe on that beautiful shore,
> I shall see Jesus, that will be my joy,
> In that bright home far away.
>
> My home is in heaven, there'll be no parting there,
> All will be happy, glorious, bright and fair
> There'll be no sorrow, there will be no tears
> In that bright home far away.

Heaven for me will be my final Home, a Place of Unity, re-uniting and love, no more tears, sorrow or pain, and God himself will be there!

Major Brian Raybould
The Salvation Army Social Services in Westminster

'Away from the world's problems. I have gone through life with a deformed hand, this will be whole in heaven!'

'Heaven to my mind would be rather like sharing the items that we at present have difficulty in being able to afford. This would be similar to the life we lead in the Salvation Army hostel in Westminster.'

'Heaven must be timeless. Without the need to refresh our bodies by eating or sleeping, the constraints of time no longer apply. Beyond that, we are on unsafe ground. My grandmother, just before she died, awoke and said, "I have been to heaven. It is a land of flowers and I have seen my husband." Possibly the ramblings of an old lady but also possibly a glimpse of a place of peace where we shall meet again our loved one. Only one other fact about heaven is known throughout the Christian world. It does exist! After all, Jesus said so.'

Residents and Staff
Salvation Army Hostel, Westminster

The real trouble about getting your eternal reward is that you just might get it in the neck in *the other place* as well. If you believe the *good* will get what's coming to them – then you have to believe it's ditto for the *baddie*. Otherwise, it doesn't matter if you're Genghis Khan or St Anthony, you're going UP.

I've always thought that heaven was here, and hell, too. And, like the rest of life, *who gets which* is pretty arbitrary. I've been lucky – my heaven is on earth.

Terry Wogan

The common version of the Lord's Prayer is part of the Sermon on the Mount (Matthew 6:9-13). It contains the request that 'thy Kingdom come, thy will be done on earth as it is in heaven.' Even for non-Christians it is not difficult to share Christ's hope that eventually the supreme bliss of God's Kingdom might be extended to embrace the world as it is believed to do in heaven.

Our concept of heaven originates in the prehistoric age. Early mankind believed that controlling the world were guardian spirits who lived way above their reach in the sky and antithetical demons who lived in the dark depths under the surface of the earth and who were responsible for death, disease, famine, plague, etc. As humans evolved they redefined heaven and hell as metaphysical concepts, heaven being where eternal joy emanated from the creator and where only good prevails.

An early example of the metaphysical notion of heaven can be found in the Iranian prophet's hymns composed about 1500 BC. The Gothic Avestan prayer of Zoroaster reads: 'May the acts of the Wise One spread, the Supreme Power's Kingdom be established over the world and the enlightened one become the guardian of the rightful oppressed.'

Shahrokh R. Vafadari
A Zoroastrian

I think heaven is a very cloudy, peaceful and quiet resting place for souls of the dead that have done more good than bad on earth. Heaven is called Bahest. I think three days after when a person dies and is buried, the person then goes to the Chinvat Bridge (Bridge of judgement) and is judged by the goodness and badness the person's done. If they have done more good than bad they go to Bahest (heaven) and more bad than good they go to Dozakh (hell) and if they have done the equal amount of good and bad they go to Hamastagan, in this place there is neither much happiness nor much sorrow.

Zubin, aged 12
a Zoroastrian boy

Whether we like it or not, we are all born on this earth as part of one, great human family. Each of us is just a human being like everyone else. Like others, we desire happiness and do not want suffering. Moreover, we all have an equal right to avoid suffering and pursue happiness.

As the end of the twentieth century approaches our world has become smaller and more interdependent. We are united by political and economic ties, linked by world-wide communications. However, we are also drawn together by the problems that confront us: over-population, dwindling natural resources and an environmental crisis that threatens the very existence of the planet that sustains us. Within the context of this new interdependence, self-interest clearly lies in considering the interests of others.

To meet the challenges that face us, we must develop a greater sense of universal responsibility. Each of us must learn to work not just for our own self, family or nation, but for the benefit of all mankind. This need to cooperate can only strengthen the human community.

The sole valid foundation for universal responsibility is love and compassion. Love and compassion are the ultimate source of joy and happiness. Once we recognise their value and actually try to cultivate them, many other good qualities – forgiveness, tolerance, inner strength and confidence to overcome fear and insecurity – come forth naturally. These qualities are essential if we are to create a better, happier, more stable and civilised world.

Although some may dismiss love and compassion as impractical and unrealistic, I believe its practice is the true source of success. Therefore, kindness is not the responsibility merely of those whose work is to care for others, but the necessary business of every section of the human community.

The most immediate challenge facing us today is that of world peace, but how can we achieve it? Beautiful words are no longer enough. We should instead embark on the difficult task of building an attitude of love and compassion within ourselves. It is evident that in order to establish genuine, lasting world peace, we must first set about creating inner peace.

In this century of rapid advancement, material development has brought with it an undue emphasis on external progress. As a result we often forget to foster the most basic human need for kindness, love, cooperation and caring. Yet, the very development of human society is founded on such a basis. So, preserving our essential humanity involves cultivating a sense of responsibility for our fellow human beings.

Once again it is clear that a genuine sense of responsibility can only come about by developing compassion. Only a spontaneous feeling of empathy with others can really inspire us to act on their behalf. Nevertheless, compassion does not arise simply by ordering it to do so. Such a sincere feeling must grow gradually, cultivated within each individual, based on their own conviction of its worth. Adopting an attitude of kindness and universal responsibility is, then, a personal matter. How we conduct ourselves in daily life is, after all, the real test of our compassion.

His Holiness the Dalai Lama

My idea of heaven on earth would be found in the countryside. An example would be a walk through Richmond Park enjoying the deer, squirrels, rabbits and birds. It would end up at Woodland Gardens, a section of the Park that is a true fantasy land. Camelias and rhododendrons of exquisite and various colours dominate the scene. Magnificent magnolia trees of all ages abound as well. The many ancient tall trees form a shelter so that the garden becomes a beautiful sanctuary for anyone seeking peace and serenity — the objectives of heaven.

Dennis Skinner, MP
Chairman of the Labour Party (1988-89)

HEAVEN
and love...

Now of that long pursuit
Comes on at hand the bruit;
That Voice is round me like a bursting sea:
'And is thy earth so marred,
Shattered in shard on shard?
Lo, all things fly thee, for thou fliest Me!
Strange, piteous, futile thing!
Wherefore should any set thee love apart?
Seeing none but I makes much of naught' (He said),
'And human love needs human meriting:
How hast thou merited –
Of all man's clotted clay the dingiest clot?
Alack, thou knowest not
How little worthy of any love thou art!
Whom wilt thou find to love ignoble thee,
Save Me, save only Me?
All which I took from thee I did but take,
Not for thy harms,
But just that thou might'st seek it in My arms.
All which thy child's mistake
Fancies as lost, I have stored for thee at home:
Rise, clasp My hand, and come.'

Halts by me that footfall:
Is my gloom, after all,
Shade of His hand, outstretched caressingly?
'Ah, fondest, blindest, weakest,
I am He whom thou seekest!
Thou dravest love from thee, who dravest Me.'

Francis Thomspon, *The Hound of Heaven*

I seem to have loved you in numberless forms, numberless times,
In life after life, in age after age forever.
My spell-bound heart has made and re-made the necklace of songs
That you take as a gift, wear round your neck in your many forms
In life after life, in age after age forever.

Whenever I hear old chronicles of love, its age-old pain,
Its ancient tale of being apart or together,
As I stare on and on into the past, in the end you emerge
Clad in the light of a pole-star piercing the darkness of time:
You become an image of what is remembered forever.

You and I have floated here on the stream that brings from the fount
At the heart of time love of one for another.
We have played alongside millions of lovers, shared in the same
Shy sweetness of meeting, the same distressful tears of farewell –
Old love, but in shapes that renew and renew forever.

Today it is heaped at your feet, it has found its end in you,
The love of all man's days both past and forever:
Universal joy, universal sorrow, universal life,
The memories of all loves merging with this one love of ours –
And the songs of every poet past and forever.

Rabindranath Tagore, *Selected Poems*

'We sometimes give ourselves to hate in masquerade
  and only think it love.
And all our lives we sing the song we thought was right.
The Canyon of the Damned is filled with singers who
  thought they knew a love song...
Listen while I sing for you a song of love.'

He began the melody so vital to the dying men
around him.
'In the beginning was the song of love...

She listened and knew for the first time she was hearing
  all of love there was.
Her eyes swam when he was finished.
She sobbed and sobbed in shame.
'Forgive me, Father-Spirit, for I am sinful and undone...
for singing weary years of all the wrong words...'

The Singer touched her shoulder and told her
of the joy that lay ahead if she could learn the
music he had sung.

He left her in the street and walked away, and as he left
  he heard her singing his new song.
And when he turned to wave the final time he saw her
  shaking her head to a friendship buyer.
She would not take his money.

And from a distance, the Singer heard her use
his very words.

'Are you betrothed?' the buyer asked her.
'No, only loved' she answered.
'And do you pay for love?'
'No, but I owe it everything.'

Calvin Miller, *The Singer*
Given by a resident of St Joseph's Hospice, Hackney, London

Saint Benedict's sister, Scholastica, who had been consecrated to almighty God in early childhood, used to visit her brother once a year. On these occasions he would go down to meet her in a house belonging to the monastery, a short distance from the entrance.

For this particular visit he joined her there with a few of his disciples and they spent the whole day singing God's praises and conversing about the spiritual life.

When darkness was setting in, they took their meal together and continued their conversation at table until it was quite late. Then the holy nun said to him, 'Please do not leave me tonight; let us keep on talking about the joys of heaven till morning.'

'What are you saying, sister?' he replied. 'You know I cannot stay away from the monastery.'

At her brother's refusal, Scholastica folded her hands on the table and rested her head upon them in earnest prayer. When she looked up again, there was a sudden burst of lightning and thunder, accompanied by such a downpour that Benedict and his companions were unable to set foot outside the door.

Realizing that he could not return to the monastery in this terrible storm, Benedict complained bitterly. 'God forgive you, sister,' he said. 'What have you done?'

Scholastica simply answered, 'When I appealed to you, you would not listen to me. So I turned to my God and he heard my prayer. Leave now if you can. Leave me here and go back to your monastery.'

This of course he could not do. He had no choice now but to stay, in spite of his unwillingness. They spent the entire night together and both of them derived great profit from the holy converse they had about the interior life.

Three days later as he stood in his room looking up towards the sky, the man of God beheld his sister's soul leaving her body and entering the court of heaven in the form of a dove.

The Dialogues of St Gregory the Great
St Scholastica was born at Norcia, Italy about 480.
She followed Benedict to Monte Cassino, where she died about the year 547.

A world redeemed; a world in which a love more powerful than sin and death has been manifested. This love is always present in it and never ceases acting in it.

This love is the *ultimate reality*.

Not only does it reveal the prospect of a fullness of life and goodness as the final end and meaning of the existence of man in God, but even in the world, *this* world, this love never ceases to transform the hearts and acts of man – of living man, of sinful man.

Our world is situated in time. It never ceases to tend to its end. But as long as it exists, this love, which is also merciful, will work tirelessly to make this human world ever more human.

Pope John Paul II
in conversation with André Frossard, *Be Not Afraid*

God who is love,
as abiding in us,
gave us love, that
we can love each other.

His Holiness Shenouda III
Pope of Alexandria and Patriarch of the See of St Mark

The love then that brought Christ down from heaven to earth, lifted Stephen from earth to heaven. The love that showed itself first in the king, shone forth next in the soldier. And Stephen, so as to deserve to win the crown – which is what his name means – had love as his weapon and by it was everywhere victorious. Through love of God and through love of his neighbour he prayed for those who were stoning him.

Trusting in the strength of love he overcame the cruel raging of Saul, and so won for himself as a companion in heaven, the man who had been his persecutor on earth. This holy and untiring love ardently desired to acquire as converts by his prayers those whom he had been unable to convert by argument.

And now Paul rejoices with Stephen, with Stephen he enjoys the brightness of Christ; he exults with Stephen, he reigns with Stephen.

What a really true life must there be now, brethren, where Paul is not put to confusion although he killed Stephen, but where, instead, Stephen rejoices in the fellowship of Paul; for in both of them love itself rejoices. And in both of them love deserved to inherit the kingdom of heaven.

Love, therefore, is the origin and source of all good things; it is a most excellent defence, the road that leads to heaven. Whoever walks in love can neither stray nor be afraid. Love guides, love protects, love leads to the end.

Christ our Lord, brethren, set up for us this ladder of love, and by it every Christian can climb to heaven. You must, therefore, keep a firm hold on love, you must show it to one another, and by progress in it climb up to heaven.

St Fulgentius of Ruspe, *Sermons*

A Prayer

One thing I know, life can never die,
    Translucent, splendid, flaming like the sun.
Only our bodies wither and deny
    The life force when our strength is done.

Let me transmit this wonderful fire,
    Even a little through my heart and mind,
Bringing the perfect love we all desire,
    To those who seek, yet blindly cannot find.

We each give to the world as much of the life force as can flow uninhibited through our confining bodies. This is our task, the reason we exist, to transmit the godhead through us. How poorly we succeed, and how much more successful we could be!

Dame Barbara Cartland

'This is my commandment, that you love one another as I have loved you.' Do you perceive that the love of God is interwoven with ours, like a kind of cord binding it together? That is why Christ at one time spoke of two commandments; at another, one. For it is not possible for him who is receptive to the love of God not to possess the other kind of love. In one place Scripture says: 'On this depend the Law and the Prophets.' And in another: 'Whatever you would that men should do to you, even so do you also to them; for this is the Law and the Prophets.' Also: 'Love is the fulfilment of the law.' This He was saying here, too. If abiding with Him is the result of our love of Him, and our love of Him is manifested by keeping His commandments, and the commandment is that we love one another – therefore, our love for one another results in abiding in God.

Moreover, He did not merely say that we should have love for one another, but even revealed the manner in which we should do this; namely, 'as I have loved you.' Once again He was pointing out that His very departure from them was motivated, not by coldness, but by love, 'so that I ought rather to be admired for it, since I am laying down my life for you.' However, He nowhere said this in so many words, but previously, in describing the best of shepherds, and also here, in heartening them and pointing out the greatness of His love and revealing Himself to them as He is, He said it tacitly.

St John Chrysostom in *Fathers of the Church*

Born at Antioch around 349, he became
Bishop of Constantinople in 397 and died in Pontus in 407.
Because of the beauty and persuasiveness of his style,
he was called John of the Golden Mouth.

Love divine, all loves excelling,
joy of heaven, to earth come down,
fix in us thy humble dwelling,
all thy faithful mercies crown:
Jesu, thou art all compassion,
pure unbounded love thou art;
visit us with thy salvation,
enter every trembling heart.

Come, almighty to deliver,
let us all thy life receive;
suddenly return, and never,
never more thy temples leave:
thee we would be always blessing,
serve thee as thy hosts above,
pray, and praise thee, without ceasing,
glory in thy perfect love.

Finish then thy new creation,
pure and spotless let us be,
let us see thy great salvation,
perfectly restored in thee:
changed from glory into glory,
till in heaven we take our place,
till we cast our crowns before thee,
lost in wonder, love and praise.

Charles Wesley (1707-88)

Guest, I answer'd, worthy to be here:
     Love said, You shall be he.
I the unkind, ungrateful? Ah, my dear,
     I cannot look on thee.
Love took my hand, and smiling did reply,
     Who made the eyes but I?

Truth, Lord, but I have marr'd them: let my shame
     Go where it doth deserve.
And know you not, says Love, who bore the blame?
     My dear, then I will serve.
You must sit down, says Love, and taste my meat:
     So I did sit and eat.

George Herbert, *Poetical Works*

The essence of a man's faith does not lie so much in his belief and conception of God as in the depth and sincerity behind it. It is for this reason that men of different faiths and beliefs have reached a high spiritual status even though their opinions and beliefs were not the same. However, the one common factor that helped them to acquire divine status was in their willingness and ability to lose themselves in God through Love and Remembrance.

If people of different faiths can bear in mind this factor, none would claim exclusive knowledge of Truth or try to prove directly or indirectly superiority of one set of beliefs against another. The paths and beliefs are different but the goal is same. Let there be more time for loving and remembering God and less for discussion and explanations about Him for as St Bernard of Clairvaux said, 'Life is only for love and time is only that we may find God.'

Cyrus P. Mehta
A Zoroastrian believer

To love God in the most practical way is to love our
   fellow beings.

If we feel for others in the same way as we feel for our
   own dear ones, we love God.

If, instead of seeing faults in others, we look within
   ourselves, we are loving God.

If, instead of robbing others to help ourselves, we rob
   ourselves to help others, we are loving God.

If we suffer in the suffering of others and feel happy in
   the happiness of others, we are loving God.

If, instead of worrying over our own misfortunes, we
   think of ourselves more fortunate than many many
   others, we are loving God.

If we endure our lot with patience and contentment,
   accepting it as His Will, we are loving God.

If we understand and feel that the greatest act of
   devotion and worship of God is not to hurt or harm
   any of His beings, we are loving God.

To love God as He ought to be loved, we must live for
   God and die for God, knowing that the goal of life
   is to Love God, and find Him as our own self.

Meher Baba
An Indian holy man who died in 1969

When I became Speaker in 1983, my wife and I decided that we would always make available the State Rooms in Speaker's House for Receptions following the christening of children of Members of Parliament. It was on one such occasion that I met, for the first time, the Bishop of Brentwood, the Rt Rev Thomas McMahon. On hearing that my name was Bernard, he suggested to me that I might put into practice the Rule of St Bernard:

> *Notice Everything,*
> *Correct a little,*
> *Cherish the Brethren.*

That is indeed a good rule for Speakers and it has been my guiding principle during the eight years that I have been priviliged to occupy the Chair of the House of Commons. I pray that in due time I may have an opportunity of expressing my deep gratitude to St Bernard of Clairvaux – in heaven!

Bernard Weatherill
Speaker of the House of Commons

> *'Where there is heaven, there is no waiting,*
> *no travelling, no persuading;*
> *but an acceptance of being;*
> *loving and being loved that which always loved*
> *and ever will; ignorant that it was ever other*
> *thus, for it never was.'*

Cllr Marie-Louise Rossi
City of Westminster

HEAVEN

and peace...

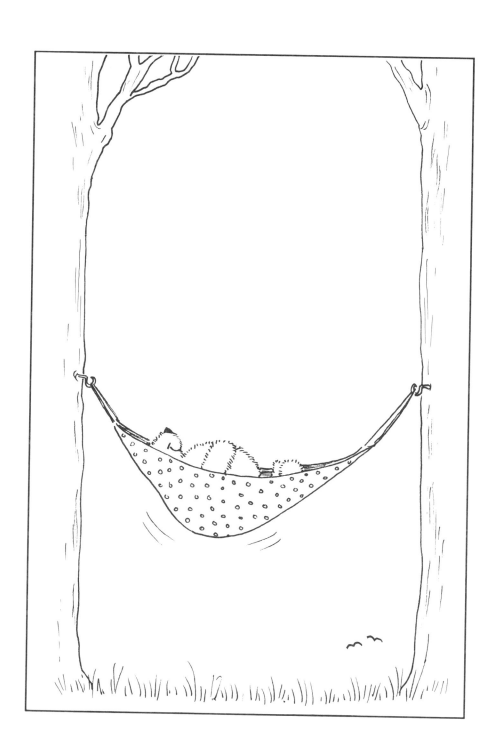

The peace of the celestial city is the perfectly ordered and harmonious enjoyment of God and of one another in God. The peace of all things is the tranquillity of order.

St Augustine, *The City of God*

We should have much peace if we would not busy ourselves with the sayings and doings of others.

Thomas à Kempis,
The Imitation of Christ

A non-violent man can do nothing save by the power and grace of God. Without it he won't have the courage to die without anger, without fear and without retaliation. Such courage comes from the belief that God sits in the heart of all, and that there should be no fear in the presence of God...

I am a man of peace, I believe in peace. But I do not want peace at any price. I do not want the peace that you find in stone; I do not want the peace that you find in the grave; but I do want the peace which you find embedded in the human breast, which is exposed to the arrows of the whole world, but which is protected from all harm by the power of Almighty God.

Mahatma Gandhi
Quoted by Elizabeth Goudge in *A Book of Peace*

The fact that the hotel I had booked into was opposite the house of Mother Teresa and her Missionaries of Charity was a coincidence, although I liked to think otherwise. I had of course decided to seek them out even if it would have meant going to the other end of Calcutta.

In the evening I went to join them at prayer from 6.30 to 7.30, when the public are welcome. The chapel is a large hall on the first floor. The altar is placed, I think deliberately, half way along the wall whose windows open out on to the street with its thundering traffic and bedlam of human and animal cries. In the space in front of the altar the sisters began to arrive and kneel, while members of the public and also perhaps some of Mother Teresa's helpers occupied the area to the right, scattering themselves unevenly.

Then that familiar, world-famous, frail little figure came in, stooping slightly and wearing the equally famous blue bordered white sari, and gestured to us to come closer to the altar. I had no hope of seeing her as I was told by her sisters in Nagaland that she was in Italy. So this unexpected apparition made me feel very lucky and happy. Then an indescribable sense of peace, serenity and clarity of existence pervaded my being in the next hour of silence which was concluded by Mother Teresa leading the recital of the rosary and prayers before Benediction.

Normally, I would have talked my way into seeing the VIP with the ready excuse that I have. But this evening I had no wish to talk to Mother Teresa because whatever I might have had to say to her would have been too trivial. I was perfectly happy. The *darshan* was enough.

But I think the most valuable information I have picked up about Mother Teresa is that even in her hour of being alone with God she does not shut out Calcutta and the world – just as the clerk at the Asiatic Society does not allow his no-nonsense, fearsome looking mother goddess Kali to crowd out Mother Teresa from his desk and heart. On his desk, under the glass pane, next to the picture of Kali, he had placed a photograph of Mother Teresa. I asked him why. And he said, in a voice breaking with pride and emotion, 'Mother gave up everything for the poor people of our city. She wants nothing back. She only wants to work for them. She loves us. She is a saint. I worship her.'

Thomas Martin
From his forthcoming book on India

In spite of all the human tragedy and evil we often face, it is always a comfort to the victims, relatives and others unexpectedly surrounded by the horrors of death and destruction to pause and discover newfound strength and faith from the kindness, sympathy and support of comparative strangers.

I can do no better than quote from St Paul's Letter to the Ephesians 6:10-18:

> *Be strong in the Lord and in the strength of his might. Put on the whole armour of God, that you may be able to stand against the wiles of the devil. For we are not contending against flesh and blood, but against the principalities, against the powers, against the world rulers of this present darkness, against the spiritual hosts of wickedness in the heavenly places. Therefore take the whole armour of God, that you may be able to withstand in the evil day, and having done all, to stand.*
>
> *Stand therefore, having girded your loins with truth, and having put on the breastplate of righteousness, and having shod your feet with the equipment of the gospel of peace; besides all these, taking the shield of faith, with which you can quench all the flaming darts of the evil one. And take the helmet of salvation, and the sword of the Spirit, which is the word of God. Pray at all times in the Spirit, with all prayer and supplication.*

Commander K.G. Churchill-Coleman
Anti-terrorist Squad, Scotland Yard

In my heaven, town centre shopping centres will be full of shops and not Building Society offices, and none of the inhabitants will understand anything about computers.

There will be a performance of a Gilbert & Sullivan opera every day and, always assuming that both Gilbert & Sullivan made it to heaven (Gilbert's temper may have been a bit of a problem), new operas will be commissioned on a monthly basis.

The operas will have to take place in the evening, because in the afternoons I shall be watching Accrington Stanley (Football Club) trounce the likes of Liverpool, Manchester United and Arsenal.

Mornings will be divided between attending a Solemn High Mass in Latin (with lots of Gregorian Chant) followed by a short meeting of the Heavenly Parliament, where Saint Dennis Skinner doesn't always have the last word.

But if all these things are not possible even in heaven, I will settle for heaven being the place where all the inhabitants do obey Christ's command to love one another.

Ken Hargreaves, MP
Conservative MP for Hyndburn and a member of the
Movement for Christian Democracy

Are we not thus far agreed?
Let us thank God for this, and receive
it as a fresh token of His love. But if
God still loveth us, we ought also to
love one another. We ought, without
this endless jangling about opinions, to
provoke one another to love and to
good works. Let the points wherein we
differ stand aside: here are enough
wherein we agree, enough to be the
ground of every Christian temper and
of every Christian action.

O brethren, let us not still fall
out by the way! I hope to see you in
heaven.

John Wesley, *A Letter to a Roman Catholic*

This letter is dated 18th July 1749
when Wesley was on a visit to Dublin.
He is the founder of Methodism.

Lord, make me an instrument of your peace.
  Where there is hatred, let me sow love;
  where there is injury, pardon;
  where there is doubt, faith;
  where there is despair, hope;
  where there is darkness, light;
  and where there is sadness, joy.

O Divine Master, grant that I may not so much seek
  to be consoled as to console,
  to be understood as to understand,
  to be loved as to love.

For it is in giving that we receive,
  it is in pardoning that we are pardoned,
  and it is in dying that we are born to eternal life.

Prayer of Saint Francis of Assisi

We all, at times, suffer from great illusions. We confuse not having peace with not being aware of the peace we possess. When our sensitive nature is all storm-tossed, we no longer perceive anything but the storm, because that occupies the most conscious part of ourselves. But that does not mean that we have lost our peace of soul, but only our awareness of it. All the same, that is enough to render these states extremely painful. This is our usual state in times of trial – an agitated sensitiveness, which makes us say: 'I have lost my interior peace'; when what we ought to say is: 'I am no longer conscious of it'.

We should get into the habit of believing in our peace of soul so long as we are not conscious of any grave fault. What is peace, after all, but God present in the soul? Provided, therefore, we have not offended Him gravely God is there. To offend Him gravely, as you know, one must actually will to do so, and we haven't come to that yet.

A Carthusian, *They Speak by Silences*

My first reaction to the question is that I don't need a heaven after life, that my idea of heaven is time with my wife here on earth. To be serious, I think that what heaven 'looks like', if it looks like anything, is relatively unimportant. Of primary concern to me is that if it exists, it should be a place of peace, a collection of inquiring minds, a community of compatible souls.

Senator J. William Fulbright
Democrat Senator for Arkansas 1945-74

He shall not judge by what his eyes see,
    or decide by what his ears hear;
but with righteousness he shall judge the poor,
    and decide with equity for the meek of the earth;
and he shall smite the earth with the rod of his mouth,
    and with the breath of his lips he shall slay the wicked.
Righteousness shall be the girdle of his waist,
    and faithfulness the girdle of his loins.

The wolf shall dwell with the lamb,
    and the leopard shall lie down with the kid,
and the calf and the lion and the fatling together,
    and a little child shall lead them.
The cow and the bear shall feed;
    their young shall lie down together;
    and the lion shall eat straw like the ox.
The sucking child shall play over the hole of the asp,
    and the weaned child shall put his hand on the adder's den.
They shall not hurt or destroy
    in all my holy mountain;
for the earth shall be full of the knowledge of the Lord
    as the waters cover the sea.

Isaiah 11:3-9

Where there is neither misery, nor pleasure, nor pain nor any obstacle, nor death nor birth; there is Nirvana (the Ultimate, the heaven).

Where there are neither senses, nor are calamity, delusion, sleep, desire, hunger there only is Nirvana.

In the state of Nirvana perfect knowledge, bliss, energy, perception, immateriality, and true yet formless existence are found.

Jain Scripture, *Niyamsara*
Contributed by Vinod Kapashi, a Jain believer

One day my children went to a funeral. A very old man – a friend of theirs, whom I did not know – had died and was being cremated. He had become very frail and ill, and more or less ceased to be interested in anything. When that happens people just give up and go. Go where? Our terminology reveals our beliefs – and prejudices.

'It was very sad,' someone said afterwards, 'very few people came to the funeral. And the officiating minister told us that, one day, we – yes, all of us – will come back.' Come back from where?

Perhaps, I suggested, neither is right: We neither go nor come back. Could it be that we are not, after all, approaching the answers to all our questions? And in this sense, the Asymptotic Fallacy suggests that all questions have answers.

Well, then let us ask once again: what is heaven? And, secondly: what are the chances that this question has an answer?

Seweryn Chomet
Lecturer in Physics at King's College, London

HEAVEN
joy and hope...

To the Salvationist, heaven is a gloriously happy place, because a Salvationist does not die, he is 'promoted to glory'. And the glory which he hopes to share is the shining glory of Christ's presence.

William Booth, the Founder, wrote in Staff Review, 1928:

> *In heaven there will be a coronation. Heaven will mean victory. The first feeling on finding myself in heaven, I think, will be the realization that will sweep over my soul that I am safe. A feeling like that of a strong swimmer who finds himself out of reach of the stormy waters, or like a racer, who after the struggle finds himself past the winning post!*
>
> *I shall have won the race. Gained the crown. Conquered the world – and myself.*

It is an exciting place to look forward to, but I'm not anxious to go there yet! There is still too much to be done for Him in service here on earth now! – As a hymn of heaven by William C Piggott says:

> *O fuller, sweeter is that life,*
> *And larger, ampler is the air;*
> *Eye cannot see or heart conceive*
> *The glory there.*

General Eva Burrows
International Leader of the Salvation Army

I confess, most noble lady, that when I consider the divine goodness which is as deep as the sea and as boundless, my mind seems to be lost and overwhelmed in its immensity. In return for how short and trifling a service does God summon me to eternal rest? How negligently have I sought the infinite joys of heaven to which he invites me! How remiss have I been in shedding those tears for which he is assuring me an eternal reward!

Consider again and again, most noble lady, this infinite mercy of God and be careful never to make little of it, as you undoubtedly would if you were to lament as though he were dead for one who is living in the sight of God. There he will give you the help of his intercession much more effectively than when he was still in this life.

Our separation will not be of long duration: we shall meet again in heaven. United in the assurance of our salvation, we shall together enjoy eternal happiness praising God with all the energy of our souls and extolling his mercy for ever as we share in the joys of eternity.

He takes from us that life which he gave us for a time for no other purpose than to restore it to us freed of all care and anxiety and to endow us with those benefits which have been the object of our hopes.

I have said all this in pursuance of my earnest hope that you, most noble lady, and all my family will regard my death as a joyful gift of God and that you will give me your maternal blessing as I cross this sea towards that shore where all my hopes are centred. I have said all this the more readily because there is no other way in which I can express to you so clearly the love and filial reverence which I owe to you, my mother.

St Aloysius Gonzaga
Born in 1568 in Lombardy, Italy, of the noble family of Castiglione,
Aloysius Gonzaga resigned his birthright to his brother
and entered the Society of Jesus at Rome.
While working among plague victims he was himself stricken
and died in the year 1591.

By definition our vocabulary is inadequate to describe the peace and bliss of heaven. After the pain, conflict and our propensity to sin, which are the hallmarks of our present existence, heaven is the place for reconciliation and healing. It is also the time of fulfilment. In *The Last Battle* C.S. Lewis describes life after the shadowlands of the here and now: 'The things that began to happen after that were so great and beautiful that I cannot write them. And for us this is the end of all the stories, and we can most truly say that they all lived happily ever after. But for them this was only the beginning of the real story. All their life in this world and all their adventures in Narnia had only been the cover and the title page: now at last they were beginning Chapter One of the Great Story which no one on earth has read: which goes on for ever: in which every chapter is better than the one before.'

David Alton, MP
Parliamentary Sponsor: Movement for Christian Democracy

My idea of a perfect heaven is that of a place that provides space for people: emotional space to develop their hearts and attitudes, and physical space to train and relax their muscles. I visualise a huge mirror, just slightly distorted to make one laugh at oneself, and develop a sense of humour. There should be bicycles and skipping ropes, and that mirror will show clearly that despite all efforts to keep moving we do look slightly ridiculous. Only thus can we develop patience with ourselves and others and achieve that inner glow that comes from the happy feeling of having tried to do better.

Sir Sigmund Sternberg
Chairman, Executive Committee of the
International Council of Christians and Jews

Because of our good Lord's tender love to all those who shall be saved, he quickly comforts them, saying, 'The cause of all this pain is sin. But all shall be well, and all shall be well, and all manner of things shall be well.' These words were said so kindly and without a hint of blame to me or to any who shall be saved. So how unjust it would be for me to blame God for allowing my sin when he does not blame me for falling into it.

In these words I saw the deep, high mystery of God which he will show to us in heaven. Then we shall understand why he allowed sin to be. And in knowing this we shall have endless joy in God.

The saints in heaven turn their will away from everything except what God would have them know... And this should be our will, too.

Julian of Norwich, *Revelations*

When I go to heaven I will be saying prayers and I will meet my parents. Heaven is full of happiness, and people are kind up there, it is probably the nicest place we ever saw.

Lisa-Marie, aged 9

Groucho Marx said that if a club elected him, he would know that there was something wrong with the club.

I would feel that about heaven if I arrived there on my departure from this planet. If I looked around and saw that it closely resembled the House of Lords a few years back, I would feel that somewhere along the line I had been seriously misled.

So for me, Purgatory is an essential article of faith. I don't say that I can understand what it is like, but I have a much clearer view of it than I have of what in the House of Lords they call 'the other place'.

Lord Longford

The kingdom of God is within you; it is not the external appeal of things, it is the invisible things of God that are the basis of our eternal life, whether in this world or in the world to come… rest, joy in God.

Fr Paul of Graymoor
Apostle of Christian Unity

Heaven is a place where spirits go for a holiday. Heaven is really God's house and people come to visit him.

Claire, aged 7
She is a Buddhist
at the Peerley Lodge Residential Care Home near Chichester

One does not normally pick up Shakespeare when in search of spiritual reading, but the following quote from *Henry VI* might be apposite. Let us remember that there is Anglican interest in that King's reputed sanctity.

Cardinal Beaufort and the Duke of Suffolk have been accused of the murder of Humphrey, Duke of Gloucester their prisoner, and the Cardinal lies dying in the presence of the King, the Earl of Warwick and others. Part II, Act III, Scene ii:

King: *Ah, what a sign it is of evil life,*
                   Where death's approach is seen so terrible.

                   Peace to his soul, if God's good pleasure be!
                   Lord cardinal, if thou think'st on heaven's bliss,
                   Hold up thy hand, make signal of thy hope.
                   He dies, and makes no sign.
                   O God, forgive him!

Warwick: *So bad a death argues a monstrous life.*

King: *Forbear to judge, for we are sinners all.*

Fra Anthony (Viscount Furness)
of the Sovereign Military Order of Malta

When St Thomas declared that joking and making people smile was a virtue, he was in agreement with the glad tidings preached by Christ, and with the hilaritas recommended by St Augustine. He overcame pessimism, clothed Christian life in joy and invited us to keep up our courage also with the healthy, pure joys which we meet on our way.

When I was a boy, I read something about Andrew Carnegie, the Scot who went to America with his parents and gradually became one of the richest men in the world. He was not a Catholic, but I was struck by the fact that he returned insistently to the simple, true joys of his life. 'I was born in poverty,' he said, 'but I would not exchange the memories of my childhood with those of a millionaire's children. What do they know of family joys, of the sweet figure of a mother who combines the duties of nurse, washerwoman, cook, teacher, angel and saint?' When still very young, he took a job in a Pittsburgh mill with 56 miserable lire a month as wages. One evening, instead of giving him his wage at once, the cashier told him to wait. Carnegie was trembling: 'Now they'll dismiss me.' On the contrary, after paying the others, the cashier said to him: 'Andrew, I've watched your work carefully; I've come to the conclusion that it is worth more than that of the others. I'm raising your wage to sixty-seven lire.' Carnegie said many years afterwards, 'All my millions put together never gave me the joy of that eleven lire raise.'

Pope John Paul I, *The Message of John Paul I*

My one personal posthumous hope is that for a few years I may live on in the memories of living friends and in any influence for good that I have achieved in life.

Barbara Smoker.

Barbara Smoker
President of the National Secular Society

Daniella: *It is a prayer.*

Carley: *I live down the road there.*

Annie: *My grandma, my great-grandma went up to heaven. I was very sad.*

Edward: *People live there... that's where God lives.*

Sarah: *Heaven is the clouds.*

Analisa: *Heaven is a church.*

Children aged 3-4 at St Vincent de Paul Nursery, London

When I think of heaven my faith strongly tells me that there I will see also the members of non-Christian religions, my brother Jews, Moslems, Buddhists, Hindus and others. The founders of these religions were all looking for God. We are all sons and daughters of the same ever living God who created heaven for all mankind.

When I think of death and that I shall die, I am not afraid but I rejoice because death is the gate of the true life, the door of heaven where I will see God my Saviour.

God, I thank you for all the beautiful things that exist on the earth. How much more beautiful things I will see in heaven. My life there will be full of wonder.

Abbot Vittorino Aldinucci, OSB
Former Abbot of the Olivetan Benedictine Abbey
of San Miniato in Florence

Heaven will look like it is in the clouds with angels everywhere and a throne which God sits on and a throne for Mary and when you look up it is so beautiful. And then you can do whatever you want till you want to do something different.

So heaven is what you always wanted to see.

Giles, aged 8
Chorister of Westminster Cathedral Choir School

I stood with an Ethiopian pastor on the treeless landscape of his barren country. He told me that his people were afraid of the hunger and poverty that beset them on every side despite all their heroic struggles for life. But he also spoke surprisingly of his firm belief that his country 'could be like heaven'. His words came like a gift and a challenge.

He reminded me, as few others could, of Christian hope as a present possibility. It has to do with life before death and not just in the hereafter. We must work for heaven to come on earth or we cannot expect it to come at all. The poor ask of us and give to us nothing less than this hope, and neither does God.

The Rev Michael Taylor
Director of Christian Aid, an official agency of
the British and Irish Churches working in more than
70 countries to eradicate poverty and increase self-reliance.

Heaven is the name we give to eternal life in perfect union with God the Father in our Lord Jesus Christ through the Holy Spirit. We will share the glory of Christ, and be in perfect communion among ourselves. Unity of all Christians can be pursued and achieved on earth but only be realized perfectly in its fullness in heaven, and then our joy will be complete. This will be a kingdom of justice, of love and peace. More than Simeon we will see the salvation prepared in the presence of all peoples. More than the Baptist, we will rejoice at the bridegroom's voice. During our life on earth we know in part, but in heaven we will understand fully, the mystery of salvation in God and in ourselves.

Cardinal J.G.M. Willebrands
President of the Vatican Secretariat
for the Union of Christians, 1969-1989

When I get to heaven I think it is going to be full of animals, hills, trees, singing birds. People will live together in peace. People will not fight nor kill.

Eric, aged 10

I think that it is a misty blue in heaven. There is always love in heaven and when someone dies everyone cares for them. I think that when people have finished all their births and become enlightened they be-come a dove or angel and help everyone.

Louise, aged 8
She attends the Chithurst Buddhist Monastery

HEAVEN
and faith ...

Dear Father Michael,

I've had some 'curly' requests during my life but to be asked by you to provide 'words' on the subject of heaven just about beats the lot!

Having been brought up in a church-going Presbyterian household, I have been sustained countless times by my faith in the Christian Church. 'Heaven' is something that has changed from a childhood idea of sitting about in the sky on fluffy clouds, sporting wings and singing praises to a harp and trumpet accompaniment to a haven from world turmoil and greed when our earthly life is over. I feel it is – a reward – a peace of mind for faithful stewardship.

Many thanks for your good wishes and congratulations on my retirement. The relief I am feeling at having shed the responsibility of 'delivering the goods' is somewhat 'heavenly'!

With my very best wishes.

Dame Joan Sutherland, AC, DBE, soprano, kindly wrote this letter shortly after her retirement concert at St John's, Smith Square, London in the presence of HRH The Princess Margaret.

Leon: Some people don't believe in heaven.

Sarah: And they go down to hell... that's where the devil is.

Edmund: I don't know if there is a devil.

Sarah: I go to Thursday Club and the teacher there knows.

Edmund: How does she know? It could be just something passed on from people to people.

Leon: True, but people think things are in London but when people are fixing the road and stuff, they don't see... I think they're a bit mad... like my mum!

Nicole: I think it's funny.

Edmund: Sometimes when my mum gets angry she might say, 'Oh, you fool, heaven and earth, haven't I got enough to do today' or something like that.

Denzil: It's a place where animals don't bite!

A discussion of children aged 8 at the Burdett-Couts & Townshend Foundation School, Westminster.

'Day by day, day by day,
Oh, dear Lord, three things I pray
To see thee more clearly,
Love thee more dearly,
Follow thee more nearly,
Day by day,
Day by day
Day by day...'

gozza

Day by Day by Stephen Schwartz and John Michael Tebelak from the Musical *Godspel*. Based on the prayer of St Richard of Chichester 1197-1253.

Paul Gascoigne of Tottenham Hotspur Football Club and member of the England team, kindly gave this, his favourite prayer.

All night had shout of men and cry
        Of woeful women filled His way;
Until that noon of sombre sky
        On Friday, clamour and display
Smote Him; no solitude had He,
        No silence, since Gethsemane.

Public was Death; but Power, but Might,
        But Life again, was Victory,
Were hushed within the dead of night,
        The shutter'd dark, the secrecy.
And all alone, alone, alone
        He rose again behind the stone.

Alice Meynell

For this we have need of much faith, patience, care and spiritual struggles. Yet, too, from hunger and thirsting for good with much prudence and discretion, but also from more earnest and boldness in prayer. Most men want to achieve the Kingdom of Heaven without toil and sweat. They certainly regard the saints as being blessed and desire their honour and gifts, but they do not want to participate to the same depth in sorrows, in their pain and their sufferings. Prostitutes too, and tax collectors and every man desire the Kingdom of Heaven. But the temptations and the trials are for this objective, for they will be manifest who truly love their Lord, so that they will righteously inherit the Kingdom of the Heavens.

Philokalia, volume 3

Let no one deceive himself. If any one among you thinks that he is wise in this age, let him become a fool that he may become wise. For the wisdom of this world is folly with God. For it is written, 'He catches the wise in their craftiness', and again, 'The Lord knows that the thoughts of the wise are futile.' So let no one boast of men. For all things are yours, whether Paul or Apol'los or Cephas or the world or life or death or the present or the future, all are yours; and you are Christ's; and Christ is God's.

1 Corinthians 3:18-23

I think in heaven I am going to be happy.

I think it will be a happy place and like a dream come true.

I'd like to be there because I would see my friend that has died.

David, aged 9

It all started with an invitation to a famous Catholic University which had asked me to talk to its students. Thus I started writing this prayer. Some time later I was asked to appear on a religious programme by the BBC. I wanted to reach people of all creeds, in all walks of life and, in particular, the young who are searching for ways of worship. I humbly hope that this, my prayer, will be of some value to those who seek.

To Thee whom I do not and cannot know – within me and beyond me – and to whom I am bound by love, fear and faith – to the One and to the Many – I address this prayer:

Guide me to my better self – help me make myself into one who is trusted by living things, creatures and plants, as well as the air, water, earth and light that sustain these, keep me as one who respects the mystery and the character of every variety of life in both its uniqueness and its mass, for all life is essential to its own survival.

Help me to preserve my capacity for wonder, ecstasy and discovery, allow me everywhere to awaken the sense of beauty, and with and for others and for myself to contribute to the sum of beauty we behold, we hear, we smell, taste or touch or are otherwise aware of through mind and spirit; help me never to lose the life-giving exercise of protecting all that breathes and thirsts and hungers; all that suffers.

Help me find a balance between the longer rewards and the shorter pleasures, while remaining in tune with relative values, while patiently according the passage of time its rich harvest of loyalties, experience, achievement, support and inspiration.

Help me be a good trustee for the body You gave me. No life is to do with as I will, not even my 'own', for it is like an object entrusted into 'my' temporary keeping, to bequeath back into the earthly cycle in the best possible condition for other life to continue.

Therefore, Thy will be done.

May those who survive me not mourn but continue to be as helpful, kind and wise to others as they were to me. Although I would love to enjoy some years yet the fruits of my lucky and rich life, with my precious wife, family, music, friends, literature and many projects, in this world of diverse cultures and peoples I have already received such blessing, affection and protection as would satisfy a thousand lives.

Allow me to see and to feel and to try to ponder and to understand the relationship of the unity of the trinity in all its manifestations.

Help me in all confrontations to see the 'trialogue' as opposed to the 'dialogue'. Help me so that I may decide wisely on such apportionment of pleasure and pain as may fall within my jurisdiction.

And finally, whilst begging Thee to protect me from anger and condemnation, my own of others and others of mine, allow me unpunished to indulge in my particular aversions:

Those who would exploit or corrupt for the sake or the abuse of power or money or self-indulgence – for want of a higher mode of satisfaction; from the petty bureaucrat to the ignorant and prejudiced; help them see and confess to You in themselves the error of their ways.

Enlighten them and me and help us to forgive each other.

Also with such enemies as I may possibly have, help me distinguish between the reconcilable and the irreconcilable, encourage me to seek by every means under-standing with the one whilst rendering the other ineffective, to learn from both and not deliberately to antagonize either.

Grant me the inspiration you have provided humanity and encourage me to revere and to follow those living examples who enshrine your spirit – the spirit within and beyond each of us – the spirit of the One and the Many – the illumination of Christ, of Buddha, of Lao-Tsu and of the prophets, sages, philosophers, poets, writers, painters, sculptors, all creators and artists, and all the selfless people, the saints and the mothers, the known and unknown, the exalted and the humble, men, women – children of all times and all places – whose spirit and example remain with us and in us forever.

Sir Yehudi Menuhin

If we care about being what we are said to be, if we want to realize fully what it means that people call us bishops and high priests, then we ought to contemplate continuously and deeply the example of him whom God made high priest for ever, and walk in his ways. He offered himself to the Father for us on the altar of the cross. Now from the high watchtower of heaven he constantly looks down on the actions and secret thoughts of all men, some day to repay each of us according to our works.

We have been appointed his representatives on earth. We have been granted that glorious title, the honour of that office. We now possess the temporal fruits of spiritual labour. We have succeeded the apostles and their colleagues in their position as heads of the churches. By our ministry, the kingdom of death and sin is to be destroyed, and Christ's building is to grow into a holy temple in the Lord, held together by faith and increasing holiness.

St Thomas Beckett

Thomas Beckett was born in London in 1118 and went on to become
Chancellor of England and Archbishop of Canterbury.
He assiduously defended the rights of the Church against King Henry II,
whose knights finally murdered the saint in his cathedral in 1170.
The above text is taken from his letters.

Heaven is God's dwelling place. In heaven there is no chaos, no sorrow, no tears, no pain. In God's presence there are all 'pleasures' that will never end (Psalm 16:11). It is everlasting, never-ending joy and bliss.

Wherever you are bow your head (to show reverence), close your eyes (to avoid distraction) and say this (either in your heart or out loud):

Heavenly Father, I have sinned against you and I am truly sorry for my sins. Wash away all my sins by Jesus' blood. I acknowledge that he is your one and only Son. I now invite Jesus to live in my heart as my Lord and Saviour. I welcome your Holy Spirit. As best as I know how I give you my life. In Jesus' name, Amen.

If you prayed that prayer and meant it with all your heart, I promise you – you will go to heaven when you die. All this is based on God's own word. His honour is at stake. He will keep his word. You need not fear. If you and I don't meet on earth I will see you in heaven.

Anonymous

I am a scientist and a person – yes, it is possible to be both.

Let me first write as a person. To my mind one of the most extraordinary things about the early Christians was the way that they went on and on about the Day of the Lord. (This was an Old Testament idea, of course; it had to be, since the New was not yet written.) This was their idea of heaven: not the vague blue-white-and-gold drabness that seems to be in the mind of more modern man, but an exciting future *dénouement* in which the existing cruel corruption of the world would be put right by none less than righteous God himself, and where Jesus would be installed as the everlasting ruler. This was Good News, and the believers took delight in spreading it around. They also took awesome risks, since their message was so often mistaken for some kind of attempt at a political revolution. Their unshakable conviction that God will ultimately usher in the new heaven and the new earth where people will matter once again, and that the world needed to hear, made them more than equal to any threat of persecution that anyone might throw at them. For myself, I too believe that people matter, and that it is not enough to believe only in this world.

As a scientist, I have to say that my message is: beware of the scientist! It is extraordinary how easy it is to believe that because someone is technically competent they are thereby fit to pronounce on ultimate issues. We worship Science (whoever she may be) too much. Perhaps we are really worshipping ourselves, since Science is so often thought to be the achievement of men and women. But think. If God is really there, we know less about him than a brick of St Paul's Cathedral knows about Christopher Wren. A mechanic may know a Honda-Williams racing car in perfect detail, and yet not know that it has been constructed for Nigel Mansell. We now know far more of the Universe than has ever been known: does that *really* entitle us to assert that God is dead and that the Universe exists for nothing and for no one in particular? And that therefore the new Heaven and the new Earth is to be ruled out? Who is kidding whom? Beware the Disingenuous Scientist!

J.L. Martin
Department of Physics, King's College, London

The fellowship which we are given with God in Christ here and now to be lived out in obedience and suffering is not to be limited to this world. It is to be fulfilled in the world to come at the 'end of the age'. Time will be no more for we shall be caught up into the ceaseless and eternal life of God which is both perfect activity and perfect rest.

In Christ we are to be occupied in the perfect exercise of the whole of our being to the glory of God. We shall forget ourselves in him yet we shall be truly ourselves, expressing with all the saints what is the breadth and length and height and depth of the love of Christ which surpasses knowledge that we may be filled with all the fullness of God.

+ Graham

Bishop Graham Leonard, *The Gospel is for Everyone*
Former Bishop of London

Heaven will be happy, no guns, no Gulf crisis.
When I get to heaven I will be happy and there will be no arguments.
I think of happiness, peace, sharing and caring.

Lorraine, aged 10

HEAVEN
and praise...

The prayer of Giordano Bruno,
Penny philosopher and one-time priest,
Magician by repute and heretic
By imputation, fomenter of sedition,
Boozer, braggart, fraud, and merry-Andrew
Dancing his jig upon the mountain top,
Waiting for star-fire… Oh God, if God there be!
O Christ, if they did not kill you forever
On your Calvary! O mother of Christ,
Who saw what men could do to one who heard
An alien music! Bend to me, be tender.
I am blind and deaf and dumb. And yet,
I do see visions, shout a kind of praise,
Feel in my pulse apocalyptic drums.
The visions may be false. I do not know.
The praise may be a blasphemy. Forgive it.
The drums – O God, you set my heart a-pounding!
Whisper, just once, 'Be still. You are at home
And safe!'

Morris West
Morris West chose this extract from
Act 1, Scene 2 of his verse-play *The Heretic*, which had
its first performance at St Martin's Theatre, London in 1969.

We must not come to God in order to go through a range of emotions… we must just come to God in order to be in his presence, and, if he chooses to make us aware of it, blessed be God, but if he chooses to make us experience his real absence, blessed be God again, because he is free to come near or not.

Metropolitan Anthony of Sourozh, *Living Prayer*

What can I give Him,
Poor as I am?
If I were a shepherd,
I would bring a lamb,
If I were a Wise Man,
I would do my part, –
Yet what can I give Him?
Give my heart.

Christina Rossetti

On being asked my views on heaven I cannot but call to mind the definition made well over a century ago by that famous Canon of St Paul's, Sydney Smith. He said, 'My idea of heaven is, eating patés de foie gras, to the sound of trumpets.'

If this sounds rather crazy I think a little reflection shows it to be not quite so absurd after all. The biblical picture of heaven is the great banquet, the feast in which all the saints share, and of which the earthly Eucharist is a foretaste. Furthermore, the sound of the trumpet has always been associated with judgement and the final destiny of man. Perhaps my addition to Sydney Smith would be to the effect that the trumpets one might hear would be the splendid brass of the Verdi Requiem!

Canon Christopher Hill of St Paul's Cathedral
and a Chaplain to Her Majesty the Queen

Lordship in right and in fact belongs
To God Most Gracious, Whose Goodness
And Glory and Power are writ large
On all His Creation. The beauty and order
Of the heavens above us proclaim Him.
Then who can reject His Call but those
In pitiful delusion? And who can fail
To accept, that truly knows himself
And the mighty Reality behind him?
The earth and the good things thereof are prepared
For man by his Gracious Lord, Who guards
him from hourly dangers. Who sustains
The wonderful flight of the Birds in mid-air?
Above, and below, and in mid-air can we see
His boundless Signs. We know that His Promise
Of the Hereafter is true. The spring and source
Of the goodness of things is in Him, and will
Appear triumphant when the Hour is established.

The Koran, volume 2, c.246

Moses went up to Heaven and brought down the Law.
The Law that is perfect, the Law without flaw,
At this Pentecost season he brought it, the perfect
        unchangeable Law.

        This day the Creator himself did come down
        To give to his people this might and this crown;
        With thunders and wonders and quakings the Creator
            himself did come down.

All the trees of the forest were shaken with dread,
The mountains all trembled, at touch of his tread;
Hill and forest alike were aquiver with an awful
        unnamable dread.

        'Twas then God instructed his sanctified fold
        In his ritual times and the hours as they rolled,
        For he loved them beyond other peoples and at Sinai
            named them his fold.

The God of salvation, he bore them on wings,
On wings as of eagles, for he beareth all things,
From his height in the aether upbeareth the world as
        on arms or on wings.

W.W. Simpson, *Jewish Prayer and Worship*

Praise to the Holiest in the height,
 And in the depth be praise,
In all his words most wonderful,
 Most sure in all his ways.

O loving wisdom of our God!
 When all was sin and shame,
A second Adam to the fight
 And to the rescue came.

O wisest love! that flesh and blood
 Which did in Adam fail,
Should strive afresh against their foe,
 Should strive and should prevail;

And that a higher gift than grace
 Should flesh and blood refine,
God's presence and his very self,
 And Essence all divine.

O generous love! that he who smote
 In man for man the foe,
The double agony in man
 For man should undergo;

And in the garden secretly,
 And on the Cross on high,
Should teach his brethren, and inspire
 To suffer and to die.

Praise to the Holiest in the height,
 And in the depth be praise,
In all his words most wonderful,
 Most sure in all his ways.

Cardinal John Henry Newman (1801-1890)

Although, Margaret, I know well that my wickedness has been such that I know myself well worthy that God should let me slip, yet can I not but trust in his merciful goodness that as his grace has strengthened me hitherto and made me content in my heart to lose goods, land, and life too, rather than swear against my conscience... I cannot, I say, therefore mistrust the grace of God. His grace shall give me that strength to take it patiently, and peradventure somewhat gladly too, whereby his high goodness shall make it serve for release of my pain in purgatory, and over that for increase of some reward in heaven.

Mistrust him, Meg, I will not though I feel myself faint. Yea, and though I should feel my fear even at point to overthrow me too, yet shall I remember how Saint Peter with a blast of a wind began to sink for his faint faith, and shall do as he did, call upon Christ and pray him to help. And then I trust he shall set his holy hand upon me, and in the stormy seas, hold me up from drowning.

And finally, Margaret, this I know very well that without my fault he will not let me be lost. I shall therefore with good hope commit myself wholly to him. And if he suffer me for my faults to perish yet shall I then serve for a praise of his justice. But in good faith, Meg, I trust that his tender pity shall keep my poor soul safe and make me commend his mercy. And therefore, mine own good daughter, never trouble thy mind, for anything that ever shall keep me in this world. Nothing can come but that which God wills.

St Thomas More

Thomas More was born in the year 1477. He studied at the University of Oxford, married and had a son and three daughters. He was appointed Chancellor of the kingdom. He wrote a number of works about civil affairs and in defence of religion. He resisted the king, Henry VIII, on the question of dissolving his marriage and on the king's orders he was executed on 6 July 1535. The above text is from a letter to his daughter, written while he was in prison.

I think heaven is peaceful and I also think that God sits there and takes in everything and everyone.

Yvonne, aged 14

Heaven is a nice place for all the good and bad and everything else.

Karen, aged 15

My views of heaven is that I do believe in heaven, that good people go to heaven and that bad people go to hell. I believe that God is now watching over us through all bad and good. God will forgive us for what we have done. I know that I shall go to heaven and I will be with my family, I won't be alone.

Zoe, aged 15

Heaven is whatever you want it to be. Nothing is pretence, the real thing isn't hidden by glamour.

Megan, aged 15

Heaven is: being happy. I think it would be the same as down here, but a few million feet in the air.

Lisa, aged 14

I think of heaven as a place where people go and talk about things with Jesus. Sometimes nice things, sometimes nasty things, impossible things and things that can be done to make the world a better atmosphere to live in.

Karen, aged 14

When you arrive at heaven I imagine I would be taken to a large white room where all my family will be, and that is the room we share and live in. I imagine it to be a perfect place with no problems to worry about, and where everybody is a friend.

Christine, aged 15

The Blackbrook House Community School, St Helens, Merseyside

HEAVEN
and sacrifice...

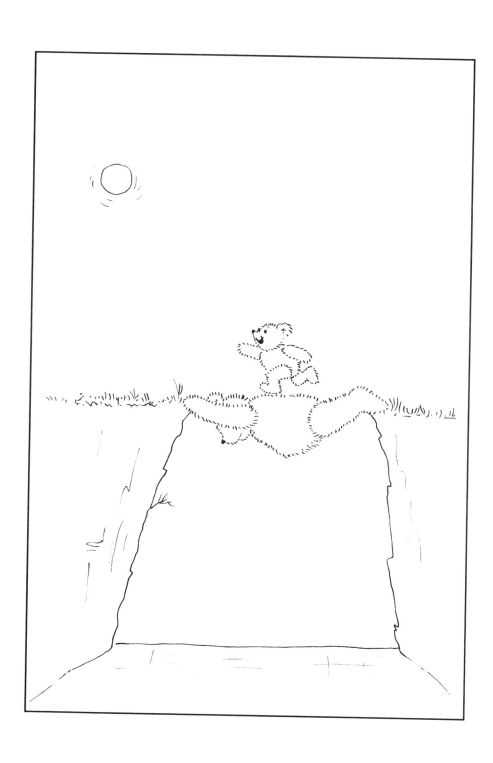

O God, grant me the serenity
to accept the things I cannot change,
the courage to change the things I can,
and the wisdom to know the difference.

His Serene Highness Rainier III
The Prince Sovereign of Monaco chose this prayer.

And when the hour came, Jesus sat at table, and the apostles with him. And he said to them, 'I have earnestly desired to eat this passover with you before I suffer; for I tell you I shall not eat it until it is fulfilled in the kingdom of God.' And he took a cup, and when he had given thanks he said, 'Take this, and divide it among yourselves; for I tell you that from now on I shall not drink of the fruit of the vine until the kingdom of God comes.' And he took bread, and when he had given thanks he broke it and gave it to them, saying, 'This is my body which is given for you. Do this in remembrance of me.' And likewise the cup after supper, saying, 'This cup which is poured out for you is the new covenant in my blood.'

Luke 22:14-20

Of Courtesy, it is much less
Than Courage of Heart or Holiness,
Yet in my Walks it seems to me
That the Grace of God is in Courtesy.

On Monks I did in Storrington fall,
They took me straight into their Hall;
I saw Three Pictures on a wall,
And Courtesy was in them all.

The first the Annunciation;
The second the Visitation;
The third the Consolation,
Of God that was Our Lady's Son.

The first was of Saint Gabriel;
On Wings a-flame from Heaven he fell;
And as he went upon one knee
He shone with Heavenly Courtesy.

Our Lady out of Nazareth rode –
It was Her month of heavy load;
Yet was Her face both great and kind,
For Courtesy was in Her Mind.

The third it was our Little Lord,
Whom all the Kings in arms adored;
He was so small you could not see
His large intent of Courtesy.

Our Lord, that was Our Lady's Son,
Go bless you, People, one by one;
My Rhyme is written, my work is done.

Hilaire Belloc, *Sonnets & Verse*

What right have you to enter heaven? Every man and woman who has ever lived will have to answer that question. A woman who had just experienced a death in her family told me she felt such an urgency to share Christ with someone that when a repairman came to fix the furnace she backed him up against the wall and said, 'If that furnace had blown up in your face and you had died, would you know for certain where you would spend eternity?' The repairman was so startled he forgot to leave a bill.

The Heidelberg Catechism, originally written in 1563 and used by Christians of many backgrounds, was a favourite of my father-in-law. On his study wall he had the first question and answer of the Heidelberg Catechism framed, which reads:

Q. What is your only comfort, in life and in death?

A. That I belong – body and soul, in life and death – not to myself but to my faithful Saviour, Jesus Christ.

Many people are deceived by Satan into thinking that God is a vengeful taskmaster, ready to send to hell all those who offend him. They can see no hope. True, God does hate sin but he loves the sinner. Since we are all sinners, our only right for admission to heaven lies in the provision God made for our sins: his Son, Jesus Christ. 'For God so loved the world that he gave his one and only Son, that whoever believes in him shall not perish but have eternal life' (John 3:16).

Dr Billy Graham, *Facing Death and the Life After*

For I have learned, in whatever state I am, to be content. I know how to be abased, and I know how to abound; in any and all circumstances I have learned the secret of facing plenty and hunger, abundance and want.

I can do all things in him who strengthens me. (Philippians 4:11-13)

Cliff Richard OBE

Be kind and merciful. Let no one ever come to you without coming away better and happier. Be the living expression of God's kindness: kindness in your face, kindness in your eyes, kindness in your smile, kindness in your warm greeting.

In the slums we are the light of God's kindness to the poor. To children, to the poor, to all who suffer and are lonely, give always a happy smile — Give them not only your care, but also your heart.

Mother Teresa
Quoted in *Something Beautiful for God* by Malcolm Muggeridge

I will see you in heaven

In this life we are all imprisoned whether by laws, just or unjust, mental or physical disability, personal circumstances of deprivation and misery or our own imperfect character. Heaven is a state of bliss in which all are free from these shackles and prison has no meaning. On earth, as Christ taught, we can always do more to bring heaven closer to prisoners.

Keith Best
Director of Prisoners Abroad, a national charity
for the welfare of British residents who are detained overseas.

To me heaven is the Vision of God, a continual unfolding of the mystery of God. Being more and more absorbed into God, becoming part of His Goodness and Love, bringing great joy and understanding. Heaven cannot be comprehended here. The eye has not seen it. All the beauty and love that we know here is only a pale image of the beauty and love of God in heaven.

Sister Elizabeth, DC

– 96 –

It is rather embarrassing to be asked about heaven. I'm not too sure to be honest, that I've ever been too bothered about heaven.

In my head the idea that there will be a place or a state or something in which all tears will be wiped away, the crippled made whole, justice at last done, misunderstandings sorted out, friendships reunited and where I will see, not just the wonders, but the source of all the wonders, is firmly fixed.

But in my heart I can't imagine all this and I don't feel for it as I feel for the return of someone I love, or for a coming hot holiday or for a walk on a sunny day on the hilltops.

One reason I suppose for this is that my heaven is not somewhere else. It is here but buried. Its shape has yet to be made clear. Heaven is the Kingdom and the Kingdom has to be built. That means effort, not just hanging around. It means using whatever talents one has been given to try to build a community of people and world that reflects, in part at least, the ideas of love and justice that God has put into our hearts.

That is enough for me at the moment. I do not doubt that road signs point to places that really exist and that they will eventually appear. But right now I'm rather busy with the journey.

Bruce Kent
Vice President of Campaign for Nuclear Disarmament
and of Pax Christi

I will see you in heaven

The closest vision I have of heaven is dreaming. The sort of dreams that people have when they see what seems like an impossible situation and they can dream of a solution. Martin Luther King had a dream of 'black and white as one' in the United States and gave his life in working for that dream. I suppose anyone who has such a dream, vision of heaven, can only give their hearts to work for it. Archbishop Romero dreamt of a time of justice for the people of El Salvador and gave his life for that dream. Don Quixote whose dreams were like tilting at windmills, is celebrated in the song 'To dream the impossible dream' from the musical *Man of La Mancha*.

But dreams do come true – when a people regain their freedom from a despot or dictator, when a community wins the right to its land and secures its future then the signs of God's kingdom, the Kingdom of Heaven, are made a fraction more visible in the world. When the Berlin Wall came tumbling down, when Nelson Mandela was freed from his incarceration, dreams came true, the innermost yearnings were realized, and we glimpsed a tiny fragment of heaven.

I feel I've come closest to heaven when I've met people, some of the poorest of the poor, who are struggling for justice against enormous odds. But holding tenaciously to their dream and gradually and precariously turning it into a reality. It's the grace of God in life. It's heaven on earth for me.

To dream the impossible dream,
To fight the unbeatable foe,
To bear with unbearable sorrow,
To run where the brave dare not go.

To right the unrightable wrong,
To love pure and chaste from afar,
To try when your arms are too weary,
To reach the unreachable star!

This is my quest, to follow that star,
No matter how hopeless, no matter how far;
To fight for the right without question or pause,
To be willing to march into hell for a heavenly cause!
And I know, if I'll only be true
To this glorious quest, that my heart will lie peaceful and calm,
When I'm laid to my rest,
And the world will be better for this;
That one man, scorned and covered with scars,
Still strove with his last ounce of courage,
To reach the unreachable star.

Julian Filochowski
Director, Catholic Fund for Overseas Development

HEAVEN
and its Mother, Mary...

Magnificat

And Mary said:
'My Soul magnifies the Lord,
and my spirit rejoices in God my Saviour,
for he has regarded the low estate of his handmaiden.
For behold, henceforth all generations will call me blessed;
for he who is mighty has done great things for me,
and holy is his name.
And his mercy is on those who fear him
from generation to generation.
He has shown strength with his arm,
he has scattered the proud in the imagination of their hearts,
he has put down the mighty from their thrones,
and exalted those of low degree;
he has filled the hungry with good things,
and the rich he has sent empty away.
He has helped his servant Israel,
in remembrance of his mercy,
as he spoke to our fathers,
to Abraham and to his posterity for ever.'

Luke 1:46-55

Let us ask our Lady to make our hearts 'meek and humble' as her Son's was. It is so very easy to be proud and harsh and selfish, so easy; but we have been created for greater things. How much we can learn from our Lady! She was so humble because she was all for God. She was full of grace. Tell our Lady to tell Jesus, 'They have no wine,' the wine of humility and meekness, of kindness and sweetness. She is sure to tell us, 'Do whatever he tells you.' Accept cheerfully all the chances he sends you. We learn humility through accepting humiliations cheerfully.

Mother Teresa
Quoted in *Something Beautiful for God* by Malcolm Muggeridge

Mary the Dawn
  but Christ the perfect Day.
Mary the gate,
  but Christ the heavenly Way.
Mary the Root,
  but Christ the mystic Vine.
Mary the Grape,
  but Christ the sacred Wine.
Mary the Corn-sheaf,
  Christ the Living Bread.
Mary the Rose-tree
  Christ the Rose blood-red.
Mary the Fount,
  but Christ the cleansing Flood.
Mary the Chalice,
  Christ the saving Blood.
Mary the Beacon,
  Christ the haven's Rest.
Mary the Mirror,
  Christ the Vision blest.

Anonymous

Mary,
by love's sacrifice,
your heart is pierced.

Mary,
by love's generosity,
you are emptied.

Mary,
in temptation
may we imitate your obedience.

Mary,
in the hour of trial
may we know
the love you gazed upon
at Calvary.

Frank Topping, *An Impossible God*

Beneath the shelter of your tender compassion
we flee for refuge, Mother of God!
Do not overlook my supplications in adversity,
but deliver us out of danger;
for you alone are chaste and blessed.

Earliest known invocation of Mary, c 360 AD
From *An Ecumenical Office of Mary, the Mother of Jesus*

Hail, Queen of heav'n, the ocean star,
        Guide of the wand'rer here below:
Thrown on life's surge, we claim thy care —
        Save us from peril and from woe.
            Mother of Christ, star of the sea,
            Pray for the wanderer, pray for me.

O gentle, chaste, and spotless Maid,
        We sinners make our prayers through thee;
Remind thy Son that he has paid
        The price of our iniquity.
            Virgin most pure, star of the sea,
            Pray for the sinner, pray for me.

Sojourners in this vale of tears,
        To thee, blest advocate, we cry;
Pity our sorrows, calm our fears,
        And soothe with hope our misery.
            Refuge in grief, star of the sea,
            Pray for the mourner, pray for me.

And while to him who reigns above,
        In Godhead One, in Persons Three,
The source of life, of grace, of love,
        Homage we pay on bended knee;
            Do thou, bright Queen, star of the sea,
            Pray for thy children, pray for me.

John Lingard (1771-1851)

In 1983, the Methodist Church published a new, authorized hymn book, *Hymns and Psalms*, which was intended also for ecumenical use. Methodists have traditionally sung their faith, as well as confessing it in the classic creeds of the Church. It is significant, then, that the new book included, for the first time, a number of hymns on Mary, the Mother of the Lord.

These included the Basque Carol of the Annunciation, which begins.

> *The Angel Gabriel from heaven came,*
> *His wings as drifted snow, his eyes as flame;*
> *'All hail', said he, 'thou lowly maiden Mary,*
> *Most highly favoured lady,'*
> *Gloria!*

There is also a hymn of the Presentation of the Christ Child:

> *Hail to the Lord who comes,*
> *Comes to his temple gate!*
> *Not with his angel host,*
> *Not in his kingly state...*
>
> *But borne upon the throne*
> *Of Mary's gentle breast,*
> *Watched by her duteous love,*
> *In her fond arms at rest;*
> *Thus to his Father's house*
> *He comes, the heavenly Guest.*

Within the section of hymns on the Eucharist, there is Patrick Appleford's:

> *Lord Jesus Christ,*
> *You have come to us,*
> *You are one with us,*
> *Mary's Son.*

All these hymns have to do with the Incarnation of our Lord, the Word made flesh. They bring into focus the truth that whoever says 'Jesus', must also say 'Mary', because he is always and for ever, 'Mary's Son'. She it was who bore him, shaped him, loved him with the unique love of a mother. She is therefore utterly central to a religion of the Word made flesh. Jesus is born of the Spirit of flesh. She opens herself to the life-giving Spirit of

God, in conceiving her child, and co-operates with God's gracious purpose, in the complete simplicity of faith and love: 'Be it done unto me according to thy word.' In her entire openness to God, she becomes the bearer of Christ, and the channel of divine love for the world.

It all stems from Mary's response, her utter willingness to do God's bidding, co-operate with his will, put herself at the disposal of his loving purpose for all mankind. In that shattering petition of the Our Father, mind-blowing in it implications, we pray that God's will may be done 'on earth, as it is in heaven'. At the moment of conception, Mary does just that, she does her part in carrying out God's good and perfect will in this world, just as it is perfectly fulfilled in heaven.

In her response, therefore, she is the pattern for all believers, for we too are called to accept, in faith and obedience, God's loving will for us, and so by his grace become channels of his peace and bearers of Christ's love to others. As a Methodist, I am reminded, by our Lady's perfect response of faith, her whole-hearted embrace of God's will for her, of the service for the Renewal of the Covenant, in which Methodists annually share. There too the keynote is joyful acceptance of the will of God in Christ for our lives, as each one pledges himself or herself to the Lord, in the words:

> *I am no longer my own, but yours.*
> *Put me to what you will, rank me*
> *with whom you will; put me to doing,*
> *put me to suffering; let me be em-*
> *ployed for you or laid aside for you,*
> *exalted for you or brought low for*
> *you... I freely and heartily yield all*
> *things to your pleasure and disposal.*

Mary then gives us a pattern of faith, as believers. She points us to our Lord Jesus, who is always, 'Mary's Son'. And since Christians form the Body of Christ, then, in the deepest sense, Mary, the Mother of the Lord, is also – like the Jerusalem that is from above – 'the Mother of us all'.

The Rev Dr John A. Newton
Chairman of the Liverpool District of the Methodist Church
and the Free Church President of *Churches Together in England,*
and a Patron of the Ecumenical Society of the Blessed Virgin Mary.

Heaven will be where no poor people live and no sorrow takes place.

Natalie, aged 9

I will see all my old friends in heaven.

Marianna, aged 10

When I get to heaven nobody is going to be screaming or fighting.

Laura, aged 9

If somebody is sad in heaven God will cheer them up, like our parents would cheer us up.

Roberto, aged 10

Heaven will be full of happiness. I will feel good inside and full of love.

Lorena, aged 9

HEAVEN
and light...

It is, I believe, impossible to write intelligibly about heaven as such, and that for two reasons, each conclusive.

The first is the limitation of human language of all kinds to express the intense joy and ecstasy which admission to heaven will bring to the redeemed and saved as they experience once and for all time the beatific vision.

More deeply is that, even when freed from the constraints of language, our limited imagination cannot even conceive the infinitude of beauty, love, and effortless activity which presence in the heavenly court will bring.

Occasionally, in this life, one is vouchsafed a pale reflection of the reality, a faint echo of the heavenly truth. One may catch a glimpse in the infinite trustfulness and love in the face of a young child, the colour of a bird's plumage, a glorious sunset or sunrise, a wide vista of mountain peaks, snows, valleys and lakes. It may be glimpsed in the song of a robin or a lark, in a humanly made painting, poem, or melody. But these are only weak approximations to the real thing.

The best thing I know about heaven is the utterly untranslatable hymn written by poor Peter Abelard in the first years of the twelfth century which begins:

> O quanta qualia sunt illa sabbata
> Quae semper celebrat suprema curia
> Quae fessis requies, quae merces fortibus,
> Cum erit omnia deus in omnibus.*

But each stanza, as it comes, says something new and pierces the heart.

Hailsham

Lord Hailsham
Former Lord Chancellor of Great Britain

*O how great and how many are those Sabbaths
Which the heavenly court forever celebrates,
Rest for the weary, reward for the valiant,
When God will be all in all.

I often wonder whether Jesus was a man of flesh and blood like ourselves, or a thought without a body, in the mind, or an idea that visits the vision of man.

Often it seems to me that he was but a dream dreamed by countless men and women at the same time in a sleep deeper than sleep and a dawn more serene than all dawns.

And it seems that in relating the dream, the one to the other, we began to deem it a reality that had indeed come to pass; and in giving it body of our fancy and a voice of our longing we made it a substance of our own substance.

But in truth he was not a dream. We knew him for three years and beheld him with our open eyes in the high tide of noon.

And all the rivers of all the years shall not carry away our remembrance of him.

He was a mountain burning in the night, yet he was a soft glow beyond the hills. He was a tempest in the sky, yet he was a murmur in the mist of daybreak.

He was a torrent pouring from the heights to the plains to destroy all things in its path. And he was like the laughter of children.

I often think of the earth as a woman heavy with her first child. When Jesus was born, he was the first child. And when he died, he was the first man to die.

For did it not appear to you that the earth was stilled on that dark Friday, and the heavens were at war with the heavens?

And felt you not when his face disappeared from our sight as if we were naught but memories in the mist?

Khalil Gibran, *Jesus the Son of Man*

I will see you in heaven

It were my soul's desire
To see the face of God;
It were my soul's desire
To rest in his abode.

Grant, Lord, my soul's desire,
Deep waves of cleansing sighs,
Grant, Lord, my soul's desire,
From earthly cares to rise.

It were my soul's desire
To imitate my King,
It were my soul's desire
His endless praise to sing.

It were my soul's desire,
When heaven's gate is won,
To find my soul's desire,
Clear shining like the sun.

This still my soul's desire,
Whatever life afford,
To gain my soul's desire
And see thy face, O Lord.

The Divine Office

My only task is to be what I am, a man seeking God in silence and solitude, with respect for the demands and realities of his own vocation, and fully aware that others too are seeking the truth in their own way.

Thomas Merton, *Contemplation In A World of Action*

Lord my God, you who formed and reformed me, tell my longing soul what else you are besides what it has seen, so that it may see clearly what it is longing for. It strives to see more, and it sees nothing beyond what it has seen except darkness. Or rather it does not see darkness, for there is no darkness in you; but it sees that it cannot see more because of its own darkness.

Truly, Lord, this is the inaccessible light in which you dwell. For there is nothing else which can penetrate through it to discover you there. I do not see this light since it is too much for me; and yet whatever I see I see by means of this light, just as my feeble sight sees what it sees by the light of the sun, but cannot look on the light of the sun in the sun itself.

My understanding is not able to attain to that light. The light itself is too bright and my understanding does not grasp it nor can the eye of my soul look at it for long. It is dazzled by its splendour, overpowered by its fullness, overwhelmed by its immensity, confused by its extent.

I pray, O God, that I may know you and love you, so that I may rejoice in you. And if I cannot do so fully in this life, may I progress every day until all comes to fullness; let the knowledge of you grow in me here in this life, and there in heaven let it be complete; let your love grow in me here and reach fullness there, so that here my joy may be great in hope, and there be complete in reality.

Until then let my mind meditate on you, let my tongue speak of you, let my heart love you, let my mouth preach you. Let my soul hunger for you, let my flesh thirst for you, my whole being desire, until I enter into the joy of the Lord, who is God, Three in One, blessed for ever. Amen.

St Anselm, *Proslogion*

Born in the year 1033 in Aosta in Piedmont, Anselm entered the Benedictine Order
in the monastery of Le Bec in France where he taught theology to the students
while he himself quickly progressed in the spiritual life.
He then came to England where he was chosen to be Archbishop of Canterbury.
There he fought strenuously for the freedom of the Church
and was twice condemned to exile.

I will see you in heaven

In almost every religion there are descriptions about the 'life hereafter.' When speaking about the terms 'heaven and hell' in contemporary Christianity, there are many kinds of teachings and expectations written down with apocalyptic ink and human imagination, inspired mainly by some powerful writers or artists (e.g. Dante's *Divina Commedia*) and not so much by biblical material. What the biblical writings are telling us about the 'heaven' is mainly expressed by parables (concerning the Kingdom of Heaven, e.g. Matthew 13 or the Last Judgement, e.g. Matthew 25) or through Christ (mystical terms of St Paul, e.g. Romans 8, 1 Corinthians 15:35-58, 10:16-17 and 2 Corinthians 4:13-18).

And this is good. It shows that fortunately, we cannot define the 'heaven' exactly. However, God through his Holy Spirit convinces us about the spiritual world still hidden from our eyes and understanding, but already present among us. This certainty sends the people of God to the struggles of this world, keeping in mind that 'our commonwealth is in heaven' (Philippians 3:20) and making the paradoxical exhortation to our own: 'We were buried with Jesus by baptism into death, so that as Christ was raised from the dead by the glory of the Father, we too, might walk in newness of life' (cf Romans 6:4).

Attempts to define the heaven, hell or dooms-day exactly have failed since the Early Church. That's why all we need to know of heaven might be expressed by the Pauline words which refer to the hidden wisdom of God: 'What no eye has seen, nor ear heard, nor the heart of man conceived, what God has prepared for those who love him, God has revealed to us through the Spirit. For the Spirit searches everything, even the depths of God' (1 Corinthians 2:9-10).

The Rev Prof. Emilio Castro
General Secretary of the World Council of Churches

HEAVEN
and life...

Heaven will be very clean and tidy. I think there will be no motorised things including cars, boats, televisions, etc. and there will be no factories. Heaven will have lots of animals and wildlife with lots of flowers and hills.

Heaven will be very beautiful.

Philip, aged 8

Therefore I tell you, do not be anxious about your life, what you shall eat or what you shall drink, nor about your body, what you shall put on. Is not life more than food, and the body more than clothing? Look at the birds of the air; they neither sow nor reap nor gather into barns, and yet your heavenly Father feeds them. Are you not of more value than they? And which of you by being anxious can add one cubit to his span of life? And why are you anxious about clothing? Consider the lilies of the field, how they grow; they neither toil nor spin; yet I tell you, even Solomon in all his glory was not arrayed like one of these. But if God so clothes the grass of the field, which today is alive and tomorrow is thrown into the oven, will he not much more clothe you, O men of little faith?

Therefore do not be anxious, saying, 'What shall we eat?' or 'What shall we drink?' or 'What shall we wear?' For the Gentiles seek all these things; and your heavenly Father knows that you need them all. But seek first his kingdom and his righteousness, and all these things shall be yours as well.

Therefore do not be anxious about tomorrow, for tomorrow will be anxious for itself. Let the day's own trouble be sufficient for the day.

Matthew 6:25-34

When I am an old woman I shall wear purple
With a red hat which doesn't go, and doesn't suit me.
And I shall spend my pension on brandy
         and summer gloves
And satin sandals, and say we've no money
         for butter.
And I shall sit down on the pavement when I am tired
And gobble up samples in shops
         and press alarm bells
And run my stick along the public railings
And make up for the sobriety of my youth.
I shall go out in my slippers in the rain
And pick the flowers in other people's gardens
And learn to spit.

You can wear terrible shirts and grow more fat
And eat three pounds of sausages at a go or only
         bread and pickle for a week
And hoard pens and pencils and beer mats
         and things in boxes.

But now we must have clothes that keep us dry
And pay the rent and not swear in the street
And set a good example for the children.
We must have friends to dinner and read the papers.

But maybe I ought to practise a little now?
So people who know me are not too shocked and
         surprised
When suddenly I am old and start to wear purple.

Jenny Joseph
Faber Book of 20th Century Women's Poems and Plays

The New York Times
229 WEST 43 STREET
NEW YORK, N.Y. 10036

ARTHUR OCHS SULZBERGER
Publisher

May 9, 1991

Dear Father Seed,

    Until I received your letter of April 25 I had not given much serious thought to Heaven. As a journalist, it seems that most of my concerns center around the lives and fortunes of those least likely to make that particular voyage. But I cannot resist the temptation to participate in a volume entitled, 'I Will See You in Heaven Where Animals Don't Bite". So here goes.

    I have never completely convinced my-self that there is life after death and that the good will go to Heaven and the bad elsewhere. Rather, I am inclined to believe that it is how we lead our lives, and how that, in turn, is reflected in the memories of others that creates our Heaven or Hell, not in some afterlife but now – on a day-to-day basis.

    But if the Lord in his wisdom proves me wrong and welcomes to Heaven those who deserve it, I do hope that I shall be included and that, among other things, I shall renew old friendships with long-gone family pets of better disposition.

With all best wishes,

Sincerely,

I have selected this quotation from a sermon by Professor E.C. Ratcliff:

> *It is a terrible fact that when men ignore God, they cease to be human; it is a terrible fact that when they deny eternity they cannot find content in time; it is a terrible fact that when they will have none of the Heavenly City, they cannot build a tolerable society upon earth.*
>
> *To look at the saints and to see them moving slowly, often painfully, but always surely towards the Heavenly Country – that is the lesson. To look at them is to begin to see what they see. Like theirs, the eyes of our hearts too will turn towards that City which is to come. Following after them, we also shall move slowly, often painfully, but, by God's grace, surely, along the unseen highway of the spirit. The God who sends us out upon this journey that he may receive us at its end will support us all the way.*

Lord Robert Runcie
Former Archbishop of Canterbury (1980-1991)

Brothers in Christ, who know the bitter harshness of the way of the cross, do not feel that you are alone. The Church is with you as sacrament of salvation to sustain you in your difficult path. She receives much when you live your suffering with faith; she is beside you with the comfort of active solidarity in her members so that you may never lose hope. Remember how Jesus invites you: 'Come to me all of you who are weary and tired, and I will give you complete rest' (Matthew 11:28).

Every day the prayer of the Church is offered to our Lord for you, especially for those of you who are abandoned and lonely, for the orphans, for those who are weakest and poorest; those whom the Lord teaches are considered as first in his kingdom.

I now turn to the families who are living within the drama of Aids. I wish they could feel the special understanding of the Pope, who is so very aware of the difficult mission to which they are called... The loss of family warmth and concern causes in Aids sufferers the diminishment and even complete loss of that psychological and spiritual state of immunity which at times is as important as physical immunity in sustaining the individual's capacity of reaction.

While searching for effective remedies, we trust that, with the help of God, life will triumph over death and joy over suffering.

Pope John Paul II
Address to the Vatican Aids Conference 1989,
quoted from *Origins* (vol 19, no 26)

One night a man had a dream. He dreamed he was walking along the beach with the Lord. Across the sky flashed scenes from his life. For each scene, he noticed two sets of footprints in the sand; one belonging to him, and the other to the Lord.

When the last scene of his life flashed before him, he looked back at the footprints in the sand. He noticed that many times along the path of his life there was only one set of footprints. He also noticed that it happened at the very lowest and saddest times in his life.

This really bothered him and he questioned the Lord about it. 'Lord, you said that once I decided to follow you, you would walk with me all the way. But I have noticed that during the most troublesome times in my life, there is only one set of footprints. I don't understand why when I needed you the most you would leave me.'

The Lord replied, 'My precious, precious child, I love you and I would never leave you. During your times of trial and suffering, when you saw only one set of footprints, it was then that I carried you.'

Anonymous
This was kindly given by Michael, a person with Aids
and is dedicated by him to all those people who care.

Reaching the wall, Juan turned and began to pray – not for himself, but for his enemies, for the squad of poor innocent Indian soldiers who faced him and even for the Chief of Police himself. He raised the crucifix at the end of his beads and prayed that God would forgive them, would enlighten their ignorance, and bring them at last – as Saul the persecutor was brought – into His eternal kingdom...

The officer gave the command to present arms. In that moment a smile of complete adoration and happiness passed over Juan's face. It was as if he could see the arms of God open to receive him. He had always told his mother and sisters that he had a premonition that he would be in heaven before them. He would say with a whimsical smile to his mother, the good but over-careful housewife: 'I will have tidied everything up for you.' Now the moment had come, the officer gave the order to fire...

Juan, raising both arms above his head, called out in a strong brave voice to the soldiers and the levelled rifles, 'Hail, Christ the King.' Next moment he fell riddled with a dozen bullets and the officer, stooping over his body, put his revolver close to Juan's ear and pulled the trigger...

No need to have fired another shot. The soul of the young hero had already left its earthly mansion, and the happy smile on the dead face told even those ignorant men where they would find Juan now.

Graham Greene, *The Power and the Glory*
Sending his signature to authorise inclusion of this passage was one of the last acts of Graham Greene, who died on Wednesday, 3 April, 1991.

Do we get wiser as we get older, or have we just, like an old dog, learnt a few extra tricks? I am seventeen going on eighty. I have learnt, I have discovered, I have dismissed. I have led, I have been led, nose-ringed by the past. In the end we must decide for ourselves, but it is making the right decisions that counts, deciding and holding on to your own beliefs, for it is you, and only you at the end of the day, who can look after yourself. No one else really cares; you don't need glasses to see that self-preservation is on the menu. You must have the strength, the will and the determination of an ox, and you must believe in your own beliefs. Can a man preach from a Sunday pulpit and not believe? I think not, for if he does we will surely see the dust on his dog-collar. We must, in the end, look to ourselves. We can take counsel, we can take advice, but in the end we must decide, it must be our decision. This is not to say we mustn't learn – we must. We must pick the brains of those who went before us; watch, learn and listen, research and discover, but, above all, the final decision must be our own.

Moments will remain in our memory, things that we have thought valuable, stored away somewhere in those decaying memory cells. Of course, there will always be a flavour of the past, for the past is a fact, but it is the future we should be looking towards, because it is the future that will be looking back at us. It is the future that will be looking at yesterday, which is our present, and in its turn will decide whether to retain or reject. This does not mean that we should perform with one eye on posterity, but that we should perform with integrity. Youth will always impersonate until it has found its confidence and its own roots.

I am seventeen going on eighty. I will continue to learn until all ceases to function. I know that the earth turns and that the sun sets and the sun rises, but I must always remember that somewhere in the shadows there are new things to be seen.

Lord Laurence Olivier, *On Acting*

'Father,' he asked, 'will John go to heaven like you said at Mass?'

'Yes, I am sure that John is happy with God,' I replied.

The four homeless men were silent a while, thinking about John in heaven.

'But there's hell too,' another pointed out darkly.

The Catholic among the four remembered: 'There is a third place you can go. What's it called?... Pur...'

'Purgatory,' I injected.

'Yes,' he said, 'a man can go to purgatory as well.'

'There are,' the first man summarised solemnly, 'three places you can be; heaven where you are with God, and purgatory where you suffer. And hell. That's here.'

'Here?' I enquired surprised. 'Is hell in this life?'

'Yes,' he said firmly. 'This life is hell.'

The other three agreed.

**A conversation between a Catholic priest
and four homeless men in a Day Shelter in London**

Youth is not a time of life – it is a state of mind. So long as your heart receives messages of beauty, cheer, courage, grandeur and power from the earth, from man, and from the Infinite, so long you are young. When the wires are all down and your heart is covered with the snows of pessimism, then you are old and may God have mercy on your soul.

Sir Peter Ustinov
to Ingrid Bergman's family
as quoted in *As Time Goes By* by Laurence Leamen

Heaven and life

Some say that heaven is hell,
Some say that hell is heaven…

In my dome of ivory; a home of activity;
I want the answers quickly;
but I don't have no energy;
I hold a cup of wisdom,
but there is nothing within.
My cup she never overfloweth
and 'tis I that moan and groaneth.
Some grey and white matter,
(Give me the Karma Mama
a jet to Mecca, Tibet or Jeddah.
To Salisbury; A monastery;
The longest journey; across the desert.
Across the weather; across the elements,
Across the water).

Kate Bush
From her album *The Dreaming*,
taken from the song 'Sat in Your Lap'

Let not your hearts be troubled; believe in God, believe also in me. In my Father's house are many rooms; if it were not so, would I have told you that I go to prepare a place for you?

And when I go and prepare a place for you, I will come again and will take you to myself, that where I am you may be also.

I will not leave you desolate; I will come to you. Yet a little while, and the world will see me no more, but you will see me: because I live, you will live also.

John 14:1-3, 18-19

Indeed, if we follow my advice, believing the soul to be immortal, and to possess the power of entertaining all evil, as well as all good, we shall ever hold fast the upward road, and devotedly cultivate justice combined with wisdom; in order that we may be loved by one another and by the gods, not only during our stay on earth, but also when, like conquerors in the games collecting the presents of their admirers, we receive the prizes of virtue; and, in order that both in this life and during the journey of a thousand years which we have described, we may never cease to prosper.

Plato, *The Republic*

HEAVEN
death and dying...

I have chosen the following passage from a splendid book on Philippians by J. A. Motyer called *The Richness of Christ* (Inter-Varsity Fellowship 1966).

'For me to live is Christ and to die is gain.'(Philippians 1:21).

This is a very full and remarkable statement about the death of a Christian. He teaches us first about the nature of Christian death: it is 'to depart'. It is possible that this is a camping metaphor. Paul, the old 'tent-maker' (Acts 18:3), resorts to the language of his trade. In this case, death for the Christian is the end of what was at best a transitory thing, a camp-life, in which he travelled, without permanent resting-place and without sure foundation. This is to be exchanged (2 Corinthians 5:1 ff.) for the 'house not made with hands, eternal in the heavens'. Camp-life is exchanged at death for home-life with Christ. But there is greater wealth of meaning in the other possibility that this 'departing' is a 'weighing of the anchor', a 'setting sail'. Never has this been given better expression than by Bishop Moule in his comment on 2 Timothy 4:6 where again Paul speaks of his 'departure', '...that delightful moment when the friendly flood heaves beneath the freed keel, and the prow is set straight and finally towards the shore of home, and the Pilot stands on board, at length 'seen face to face.' And, lo, as He takes the helm, 'immediately the ship is at the land whither they go' (John 6:21)' (H. C. G. Moule, *A Devotional Commentary*, p. 140).

When a Christian dies all the uncertainties and dangers lie behind: the uncertainties and dangers whether of camp-life or of temporary stay in a foreign port. All the certainties and safeties lie ahead in the presence of Christ. And this, in the second place, is the blessedness of Christian death. Such a one goes to 'be with Christ'. So much about life after death is left, by Scripture, without certain description, but on this central fact there is no hesitation: the Christian dead are 'with Christ'. This is not only the blessedness to which Paul looks forward at the second coming: 'the Lord himself will descend... so shall we always be with the Lord' (1 Thessalonians 4:16 f.); 'we await a Saviour, the Lord Jesus Christ' (Philippians 3:20). As he faced what might well be imminent death this was the centre of his expectation, 'with Christ'.

+ George Carey

Archbishop George Carey
Archbishop of Canterbury

Last year's Festival of Remembrance in the Albert Hall in London suddenly seemed to have a little message for me about our death. In the centre is the large arena on which the action takes place, and round it, tier upon tier of spectators, a cross-section of the nation with the Queen at their head. The action mostly consists of displays by the armed forces, but others enter the stage too – somebody who was wounded in the war, some ex-nursing auxiliaries, a land army girl, a widow and so on. They are first announced, then enter via a short tunnel and down some steps and everybody's straining to see them, clapping and cheering as they walk across the arena.

Well, in a tiny way, I think that's a mirror of the day we enter heaven. The moment of our dying is an extremely solemn moment, it's a moment of the most profound possible meaning, not just to us but to the myriads and myriads who already inhabit heaven, who see it as a marvellous victory – of Christ who made it possible, but also of us who, too, paid a price. You could even say there's a third victory, of all those who've helped us on our way. Each person who enters heaven adds to the joy of everybody else there. So different from our attitude on earth!

Lord Cheshire, *Where's God in All This?*

I liked him.
I liked him right away.
We prayed together last night before we went to bed.

We couldn't turn off the air conditioner.
He was sniffling; so I asked him, 'Are you alright?'
He said, 'Not too good.'
I said, 'If we pray, maybe you'll be better.'

We didn't hold hands or anything.
He said he didn't know how to pray.
I told him when you talk from the heart,
It will come through no matter what you feel.
I felt a spiritual uplifting.

I think he was ready;
He had a smile on his face.
They went to get the doctor; at 6.05 he died.

He didn't die alone;
You got to acknowledge: he exists in your heart.

The Family at Christ House
By courtesy of Christ House, Washington, D.C. which is
a hospital for the homeless and
part of the ministry of The Church of The Saviour,
an ecumenical community founded in 1947.

I offer for reflection this passage from Canon Henry Scott Holland (1847-1918):

Death is nothing at all... I have only slipped away into the next room... I am I and you are you... Call me by my old familiar name, speak to me in the easy way which you always used. Put no difference into your tone; wear no forced air of solemnity or sorrow. Laugh as we always laughed at the little jokes we enjoyed together. Play, smile, think of me, pray for me. Let my name be ever the household word that it always was. Let it be spoken without an effort, without the ghost of a shadow on it. Life means all that it ever meant. It is the same as it ever was. Why should I be out of mind because I am out of sight? I am but waiting for you. For an interval, somewhere very near just around the corner... All is well.

HRH The Duchess of Kent

After these things, the saint raised his hands to heaven and praised his Christ, because, freed now of all things, he was going to him free. Indeed, that he might show himself to be a true imitator of Christ his God in all things, he loved to the end his brothers and sons whom he had loved from the beginning. He had all the brothers present there called to him and soothing them with comforting words in view of his death, he exhorted them with paternal affection to love God. Then, with all the brothers sitting about, he extended his right hand over them and beginning with his vicar, he placed it upon the head of each one. 'Farewell,' he said, 'all you my sons, in the fear of the Lord, and may you remain in him always! And because a future temptation and tribulation is approaching, happy will they be who will persevere in the things they have begun. I am hastening to the Lord, to whose grace I commend you all.'

He himself, in as far as he was able, broke forth in this psalm: I cried to the Lord with my voice: with my voice I made supplication to the Lord. He also invited all creatures to praise God, and by means of the words he had composed earlier, he exhorted them to love God. He exhorted death itself, terrible and hateful to all, to give praise, and going joyfully to meet it, he invited it to make its lodging with him. 'Welcome,' he said, 'my sister death.' To the doctor he said: 'Tell me bravely, brother doctor, that death, which is the gateway of life, is at hand.' Then to the brothers: 'When you see that I am brought to my last moments, place me naked upon the ground just as you saw me the day before yesterday; and let me lie there after I am dead for the length of time it takes one to walk a mile unhurriedly.' The hour therefore came, and all the mysteries of Christ being fulfilled in him, he winged his way happily to God.

Thomas of Celano, *The Second Life*
Quoted from *Franciscan Readings*.
St Francis of Assisi was born in the year 1182.
From being a light-hearted youth he changed,
gave up his inheritance and bound himself to God,
embracing poverty and living the life of the gospels.
He preached to all the love of God. He died in the year 1226.

Death be not proud, though some have called thee
Mighty and dreadful, for, thou art not so,
For, those, whom thou think'st thou dost overthrow
Die not, poor death, nor yet canst thou kill me;
From rest and sleep, which but thy pictures be,
Much pleasure, then from thee, much more must flow,
And soonest our best men with thee do go,
Rest of their bones, and soul's delivery.
Thou art slave to fate, chance, kings and desp ate men,
And dost with poison, war and sickness dwell,
And poppy, or charms can make us sleep as well,
And better than thy stroke, why swellest thou then?
One short sleep past, we wake eternally
And death shall be no more, Death thou shalt die.

John Donne, *Sonnet VI*

Show your eagerness to give your allegiance,
first to the Lord and then to his saints, *that
after your death they may receive you into
everlasting dwellings* as familiar friends. Give
these things your thought, make them your
purpose.

Saint Antony
Quoted from *Butler's Lives of the Saints*

Two others also, who were criminals, were led away to be put to death with him. And when they came to the place which is called The Skull, there they crucified him, and the criminals, one on the right and one on the left. And Jesus said, 'Father, forgive them; for they know not what they do.' And they cast lots to divide his garments. And the people stood by, watching; but the rulers scoffed at him, saying, 'He saved others; let him save himself, if he is the Christ of God, his Chosen One!' The soldiers also mocked him, coming up and offering him vinegar, and saying, 'If you are the King of the Jews, save yourself!' There was also an inscription over him, 'This is the King of the Jews.'

One of the criminals who were hanged railed at him, saying, 'Are you not the Christ? Save yourself and us!'

But the other rebuked him, saying, 'Do you not fear God, since you are under the same sentence of condemnation? And we indeed justly; for we are receiving the due reward of our deeds; but this man has done nothing wrong.'

And he said, 'Jesus, remember me when you come in your kingly power.'

And he said to him, 'Truly, I say to you, today you will be with me in Paradise.'

Luke 23:32-43

For your reflection I would like to suggest the following passage from "The Mishnah".

Imagine an unborn child in the mother's womb were endowed with a fully developed intellect and perfect senses. It would doubtless regard its dark, confined space within the mother as its entire world and the period of its foetal growth as its life-time.

Now imagine there were twins, and they started arguing and speculating: 'What is to become of us after we leave the womb and depart from our universe?'

Now imagine one twin has faith and claims some knowledge – by tradition or intuition – of a future life after leaving the mother, whilst the other is a sceptic, believing only what his senses and mind can perceive – only in 'this world' which he can see and feel.

The first will argue: 'I have faith, sustained by a long tradition which has come down to me, that on leaving the womb, we will enter a new life of much broader dimensions.'

But the other twin will laugh and scoff at this 'simpleton', saying: 'Only a fool can believe all these imbecile stupidities and idiocies which the mind cannot grasp.' 'And according to you,' asks the child of faith, 'what will happen to us after we leave the womb?' 'That is simple and obvious,' answers the 'enlightened' sceptic, 'when we depart from this world of ours, our food supply will be cut off and we will fall into the abyss from which there is no return.'

As they talked, the womb opened. The 'simpleton' departs first. The 'rational' twin still inside trembles with shock and grief at the 'misfortune' that befell his brother. As he bewails the loss of his brother, he hears a terrible shriek from his fellow-twin just outside the womb. The brother inside shakes with terror and exclaims: 'Woe, this is his final agonizing death cry as he gives up his life!'

And while this yet unborn twin grieves and wails over his brother's 'death', there is rejoicing and festivity in the home of the new-born. The parents and relatives begin to celebrate and greet each other: 'Mazal Tov, Mazal Tov – a son is born to us!'

Lord Immanuel Jakobovits
Chief Rabbi of the United Hebrew Congregation
of the British Commonwealth of Nations

At seven she died after a terrible accident with a grin on her beautiful face, saying: 'I bet Mister God lets me get into heaven for this.'

Anna's grave was a brilliant red carpet of poppies. Lupins stood guard in the background. A couple of trees whispered to each other whilst a family of little mice scurried backwards and forwards through the uncut grass. Anna was truly home. She didn't need a marker. You couldn't better this with a squillion tons of marble. I stayed for a little while and said goodbye to her for the first time in five years.

As I made my way back to the main gates I passed by hordes of little marble cherubs, angels and pearly gates. I stopped in front of the twelve-foot angel, still trying to lay down its bunch of marble flowers after God knows how many years.

'Hi, chum,' I said, saluting the angel, 'you'll never make it, you know.'

I swung on the iron gates as I yelled back into the cemetery.

'The answer is "In my middle".'

A finger of thrill went down my spine and I thought I heard her voice saying, 'What's that the answer to, Fynn?'

'That's easy. The question is "Where's Anna?"

I had found her again – found her in my middle.

I felt sure that somewhere Anna and Mister God were laughing.

Fynn, *Mister God, This is Anna*

I can remind you of two quotations about heaven which I particularly enjoy, both treating heaven as a physical reality rather like the park with well-trimmed lawns and flower-beds which was the dog cemetery in Evelyn Waugh's *The Loved One*.

The first quotation, delightfully incomprehensible, came from Emmanuel Swedenborg (who was moved to found his sect, according to a contemporary, when an image of Jesus Christ appeared in front of Swedenborg while he was enjoying a chop in a Ludgate Hill cookshop and said 'Eat slower'.) Swedenborg wrote: 'One of the wonders of heaven is that no one there is ever permitted to stand behind another and look at the back of his head.'

The second quotation came from the splendid old Countess of Cork and Orrery (1746-1840), bluestocking, hostess and wit, who died at the age of ninety-four. As she was gently fading away, an old servant leant over the bed and murmured, 'Take heart, my lady – in a moment or two you will be in heaven.' Milady opened an eye and said loudly, 'But I don't want to be in heaven – all that sitting about on damp clouds singing hymns!'

Frank Muir
Broadcaster, author and wit

There is a time in a patient's life when the pain ceases to be, when the mind slips off into a dreamless state, when the need for food becomes minimal and the awareness of the environment all but disappears into darkness.

This is the time when the relatives walk up and down the hospital hallways, tormented by the waiting, not knowing if they should leave to attend the living or stay to be around for the moment of death. This is the time when it is too late for words, and yet the time when the relatives cry the loudest for help — with or without words. It is too late for medical interventions (and too cruel, though well meant, when they do occur), but it is also too early for a final separation from the dying. It is the hardest time for the next of kin as he either wishes to take off, to get it over with; or he desperately clings to something that he is in the process of losing forever. It is the time for the therapy of silence with the patient and availability for the relatives.

Those who have the strength and the love to sit with a dying patient in the silence that goes *beyond words* will know that this moment is neither frightening nor painful, but a peaceful cessation of the functioning of the body.

Watching a peaceful death of a human being reminds us of a falling star; one of a million lights in a vast sky that flares up for a brief moment only to disappear into the endless night forever. To be a therapist to a dying patient makes us aware of the uniqueness of each individual in this vast sea of humanity. It makes us aware of our finiteness, our limited life-span.

Few of us live beyond our three score and ten years and yet in that brief time most of us create and live a unique biography and weave ourselves into the fabric of human history.

Elisabeth Kübler-Ross, *On Death and Dying*

Now there is light. In fact, the sun has even broken through and the large stretches of blue sky now visible behind the clusters of clouds remind me again that often what we see is not what is most enduring.

Dear father, this seems the most natural time to conclude not only the Easter celebration but also this letter. For twelve days I have been reflecting on mother's death in the hope of offering you and myself some comfort and consolation. I do not know if I have been able to reach you in your loneliness and grief. Maybe my words often said more to me than to you. But even if this is so, I still hope that the simple fact that these words have been written by your son about her whom we have both loved so much will be a source of consolation to you.

Henri J.M. Nouwen, *A Letter of Consolation*

I am afraid that I have little to say on the subject of heaven, but you might care for a quotation from the Book of Revelation – a quotation which I have often read from the pulpit – a good political quote!

'AND I SAW A NEW HEAVEN AND A NEW EARTH:
FOR THE FIRST HEAVEN AND THE FIRST EARTH
WERE PASSED AWAY.'

You will see that I did not finish the quotation – we are rather fond of the sea!

Wilson of Rievaulx

Lord Wilson of Rievaulx

When it came to the Tuesday before Ascension Day, Bede's breathing became very much worse, and a slight swelling had appeared in his feet; but all the same he taught us the whole of that day, and dictated cheerfully. But it seemed to us that he knew very well when his end would be.

At three o'clock he said to me: 'I have a few treasures in my box, some pepper and napkins, and some incense. Run quickly and fetch the priests of our monastery, and I will share among them such little presents as God has given me.' I did so, in great agitation; and when they came, he spoke to them and to each one singly.

But they were very sad, and they all wept, especially because he had said that he thought they would not see his face much longer in this world. Yet they rejoiced at one thing that he said: 'It is time, if it so please my Maker, that I should be released from the body, and return to him who formed me out of nothing, when as yet I was not.'

Then the boy of whom I spoke, whose name was Wilberht, said once again: 'There is still one sentence, dear master, that we have not written down.' And he said: 'Write it.' After a little the boy said: 'There! Now it is written.' And he replied: 'Good! It is finished; you have spoken the truth. Hold my head in your hands, for it is a great delight to me to sit over against my holy place in which I used to pray, that as I sit there I may call upon my Father.'

And so upon the floor of his cell, singing 'Glory be to the Father and to the Son and to the Holy Spirit' and the rest, he breathed his last. And well may we believe without hesitation that, inasmuch as he had laboured here always in the praise of God, so his soul journeyed to the joys of heaven which he longed for.

The Letter of St Cuthbert on the Death of St Bede the Venerable
Born near the monastery of Wearmouth in the year 673
Bede received his education from St Benedict Biscop.
He became a priest and spent his time teaching and writing.

There must be somewhere, where the children live
Who die in pain, asking their mothers why?
Some far-off place, untroubled by our tears,
Where they may travel through their stolen years
And lost maturity?

Will those, in battle or in accident
Blasted from life, no time to say a prayer,
Awaken to tranquillity, and find
The suicides, the handicapped and blind
Restored to wholeness there?

And to that country, shall we come at last,
From life, through death, come once again to live
And know at last the reason for our pain,
And those we loved and wounded, see again
And ask them to forgive?

Our childhood images may disappear –
No stern Saint Peter waiting with his keys
To open pearly gates on streets of gold,
No shining angels will their wings unfold
To greet us; none of these,

But such a peace as we have never known,
And such a light as here has never shone
Unless we glimpsed it in the afterglow
On summer Sunday evenings long ago
After the sun had gone.

O Spirit whence we came, it must be so,
It must be so, O God whom we adore!
You would not thrust us into endless sleep,
Into a nothingness so vast, so deep
That we are lost for evermore?

Lady Mary Wilson, *New Poems*

It has been my privilege to work as a hospice doctor. But what is a hospice?

The patients are in the advanced stage of progressive incurable illness such as cancer, and when they arrive at the hospice they are often frightened, anxious, and most are already aware that their life expectancy is weeks rather than months. Many are suffering severe pain or in great discomfort from other distressing symptoms. Our first duty is to gain the patient's confidence and trust by providing appropriate treatment to alleviate the physical suffering. This does not include extraordinary or excessive measures which would be quite wrong for a patient who is dying. It does require medications and nursing skills which when correctly applied will relieve physical distress while not reducing mental alertness. Fortunately, such treatment is available and is extremely effective.

Other causes of suffering must then be considered – social, emotional, spiritual. A dying patient is still a living person and the hospice aim is to enable patients to *live* until they die, and to use the remaining precious weeks to good purpose. They are frail, dependent, vulnerable and in need of that security which can only be demonstrated by love and kindness. And the most valuable thing we can give them is our time; their time is rapidly running out.

As the patient's life disintegrates, the life of the family may also fall apart and be in need of support. Even before the patient dies the anguish of grief will be evident. Grief is the price we pay for loving someone and there is no short-cut through it. It is however a particular aspect of suffering for which a firm religious faith will give great solace.

Dr J. F. Hanratty, OBE, KSG
Chairman, and formerly Medical Director,
St Joseph's Hospice, Hackney, London
and author of *Palliative Care of the Terminally Ill*

HEAVEN

in heaven...

Trades Union Congress

Congress House, Great Russell Street, London WC1B 3LS
Telephone: 071-636 4030; Fax: 071-636 0632; Telex: 268 328 TUCG

Dear Father Seed

Thank you for your letter – I enclose a small poem penned in response, together with another on Heaven and Earth. (I've always loved it).

These are sent with some diffidence, unusual for the TUC. After all, recent research has brought to light the TUC Prayer:

> 'Use us, O Lord,
> Use thy servants – even if only in
> an advisory capacity.'

Best wishes.

Yours sincerely,

Norman Willis

General Secretary

General Secretary: Norman Willis
Deputy General Secretary: John Monks
Assistant General Secretaries:
Roy Jackson and David Lea, OBE

The Bells of Heaven

T'would ring the bells of Heaven
The wildest peal for years,
If Parson lost his senses
And people came to theirs
And he and they together
Knelt down with angry prayers
For tamed and shabby tigers
And dancing dogs and bears
And wretched, blind pit ponies
And little hunted hares.

Listed Value

Abu Ben Adhem (may his doubts increase!)
Awoke one morning, still bereft of peace,
Uncertain if the Angel's list was worth
As much in Heaven as it was on Earth

after Leigh Hunt

I recall the way that spiritual exercises in childhood hovered between rigorous primary school learning by rote and bemused speculations about infinity.

I remember being tested on the three theological virtues, the four cardinal virtues, the seven gifts of the Holy Spirit, the twelve fruits of the Holy Spirit, the seven corporal works of mercy and the equivalent spiritual works. I'm ashamed to say that I've forgotten them, but at least know these days what longanimity and continency mean!

As for infinity, I saw it like this. There was a firm of furniture removers called Lamerton's in Ealing where I grew up. Their vans had a picture of another Lamerton's van on the side which had in turn a picture of another van on it, and so on. I reckoned infinity was a succession of removers' lorries.

So the heaven I grew up with wasn't foie gras and trumpets, but all those cardinal virtues and works of mercy borne along the way by an endless convoy of Lamerton's lorries.

How would I see it today? To be honest, I'm more concerned about being prepared for it than what it's like. And being prepared means not being frightened of dying. I hope I can manage that one day, and have the time to prepare myself too. To die cheerfully would be a sort of heaven.

Christopher Patten, MP
Chairman of the Conservative Party

I feel sure that many of those who have been engaged over the past twenty-five years, and even before that, in ecumenical dialogue are now together united before the throne of God. I wonder what they think now of the divisions which exist among the disciples of Christ and the obstacles to our full and perfect communion in the Lord. Through our faith in the Risen Lord and our communion with him and with those baptized into the Body of Christ we already live that new life which will reach its perfection in heaven. How much more like our heavenly home would be our life on earth if we could find again the unity of the one, holy Church of earlier times. May these thoughts inspire others, as they do me, in giving all to the work of Christian Unity.

Cardinal Edward I. Cassidy
President of the Pontifical Council for the Union of Christians

Let nothing disturb thee, nothing
afright thee;
All things are passing; God never
changeth;
Patient endurance
Attaineth to all things;
Who God possesseth
In nothing is wanting;
Alone God sufficeth.

St Teresa of Avila

I am rather hoping to see all of my friends in heaven even though one or two have been rather naughty.

I also hope that God plays cricket. Still, if the rumour is true that he is an Englishman, he is bound to. Isn't he?

Jeffrey Archer

Malcolm Williamson, OBE, composer, pianist, organist, and Master of the Queen's Music, chose this poem:

Fish (fly-replete, in depth of June,
Dawdling away their wat'ry noon)
Ponder deep wisdom, dark or clear,
Each secret fishy hope or fear.
Fish say, they have their Stream and Pond;
But is there anything Beyond?
This life cannot be All, they swear,
For how unpleasant, if it were!
One may not doubt that, somehow, Good
Shall come of Water and of Mud;
And, sure, the reverent eye must see
A Purpose in Liquidity.
We darkly know, by Faith we cry,
The future is not Wholly Dry.
Mud unto mud! – Death eddies near –
Not here the appointed End, not here!
But somewhere, beyond Space and Time,
Is wetter water, slimier slime!
And there (they trust) there swimmeth One
Who swam ere rivers were begun,
Immense, of fishy form and mind,
Squamous, omnipotent, and kind;
And under that Almighty Fin,
The littlest fish may enter in.
Oh! never fly conceals a hook,
Fish say, in the Eternal Brook,
But more than mundane weeds are there,
And mud, celestially fair;
Fat caterpillars drift around,
And Paradisal grubs are found;
Unfading moths, immortal flies,
And the worm that never dies.
And in that Heaven of all their wish,
There shall be no more land, say fish.

The Poetical Works of Rupert Brooke

Heaven in heaven

There is no need to be worried by facetious people who try to make the Christian hope of 'heaven' ridiculous by saying they don't want 'to spend eternity playing harps'. The answer to such people is that if they cannot understand books written for grown-ups, they should not talk about them. All the scriptural imagery (harps, crowns, gold, etc.) is, of course, a merely symbolical attempt to express the inexpressible. Musical instruments are mentioned because for many people (not all) music is the thing known in the present life which most strongly suggests ecstasy and infinity. Crowns are mentioned to suggest the fact that those who are united with God in eternity share his splendour and power and joy. Gold is mentioned to suggest the timelessness of heaven (gold does not rust) and the preciousness of it. People who take these symbols literally might as well think that when Christ told us to be like doves, he meant that we were to lay eggs!

C. S. Lewis, *Christian Behaviour*

In this way, however, is the Deity disposed as to existence, and the principle of life is, at any rate, inherent in the Deity; for the energy or active exercise of Mind constitutes life, and God constitutes this energy; and essential energy belongs to God as his best and everlasting life.

Now, our statement is this, that the Deity is an animal that is everlasting and most excellent in nature; so that with the Deity life and duration are uninterrupted and eternal: for this constitutes the very essence of God.

Aristotle, *The Metaphysics*

Death – it is the end of this definite and determined
world and the beginning of an endless life.
One's love does not end by death
but the door of a more important and eternal world
opens on death.

The future life begins with this present life;
the conclusion of life depends upon the worldly life.
Therefore, the future life is a result of our present life.

The Concise Islamic Catechism

They that have been beside us all the day
>*Rise up; for they are summoned to the gate.*
Nor turn the head but take a downward way;
>*Depart, and leave their households desolate.*
But you shall not depart, although you leave
>*My house for conversation with your peers.*
Your admirable ghost shall not receive
>*Mere recollected vows and secret tears.*

But on that brink of Heaven where lingering stand
>*The still-remembrant spirits hearkening down*
Go, tower among them all, to hear the land,
>*To hear the land alive with your renown.*
>*Nor strength, nor peace, nor laughter could I give,*
>*But this great wages: after death, to live.*

Hilaire Belloc, *Sonnets and Verse*

The times are nightfall, look, their light grows less;
The times are winter, watch, a world undone:
They waste, they wither worse; they as they run
Or bring more or more blazon man's distress.

And I not help. Nor word now of success:
All is from wreck, here, there, to rescue one —
Work which to see scarce so much as begun
Makes welcome death, does dear forgetfulness.

Or what is else? There is your world within.
There rid the dragons, root out there the sin.
Your will is law in that small commonweal.

Gerard Manley Hopkins

The kingdom of heaven is like treasure hidden in a field, which a man found and covered up; then in his joy he goes and sells all that he has and buys that field.

Again, the kingdom of heaven is like a merchant in search of fine pearls, who, on finding one pearl of great value, went and sold all that he had and bought it.

Matthew 13:44-46

This is the earth he walked on; not alone
    That Asian country keeps the sacred stain;
    Ah, not alone the far Judaean plain,
    Mountain and river! Lo, the sun that shone
On him, shines now on us; when day is gone
    The moon of Galilee comes forth again
    And lights our path as his; an endless chain
    Of years and sorrows makes the round world one.

Richard Watson Gilder

The intrinsic nature of all things is pure and perfect. All things, spiritual, mental and physical, internal and external, all are born, die and function according to the laws of nature – they are all aspects of the one truth. When we abandon our self-centred perspectives on life this truth is realized, and the division of life, into what I like and what I don't like, vanishes. We wake up to the fact that we have been in the midst of perfection all along but had failed to notice it. Heaven was here but we were hunting for it so hard, trying so furiously to get there, that we never gave ourselves the chance to feel its presence.

When we let go of all self-centred activity, wisdom and kindness guide our lives; our hearts are wide open, like the great sky. This brings peace – if we let go a little, we experience a little peace; if we let go a lot, we experience a lot of peace; if we let go completely, we experience complete peace. And this is not only for ourselves: our lives touch each other, therefore the peace we experience, and the wisdom and love which guide us, will radiate out to those around us.

Some find this kind of presence gladdening and inspiring, some find it irritating but this is to be expected. If I am determined to believe in my opinions and cling to fears and desires, when the light of truth illuminates that clinging I will resist. Sooner or later, however, we must recognize our unity with all things, for ultimately it's not a matter of choice. The wave cannot be separated from the sea no matter how much it might believe it is alone or special or at odds.

'Union with God', 'Enlightenment', 'Release' – these words all indicate the supreme fulfilment of our lives. They point to that realm of vision wherein, when I see you and you see me, there is only peace.

Amaro Blinkklu
The Amaravati Buddhist Centre, Gt. Gaddesden

Certainly heaven has no division bells and no whips, with the possible exception of the Recording Angel who must quite often draw three ominous lines under his jottings. I have long suspected him of setting up 'usual channels' with his earthly counterparts, for how else could they know so much about us...?

Mine is the traditional Christian heaven – cherubims, white nightgowns, harps and sweet music (forced choruses and warbled hallelujahs, says Milton's Satan rather unkindly, but presumably up there I shall warble in tune whereas down here I am tone deaf).

None of the other versions of heaven bears contemplating. If I arrived in the underworld of the ancient Greeks the first thing I should do would be to privatise the ferry service. The thought of standing on the bank while the Hades State Monopoly transported my fellow-departed one by one would make London Transport very quickly look like heaven. Anyway what would Charon do if I set up a fleet of privately operated profit-making ferries? He could hardly form a union, but there again what would his rivals do with their profits?

Worse still it might be Valhalla – eternal battles interspersed with eating and drinking. I suppose I would not really know I had left the House of Commons except the wounds would heal quicker.

As John Wyndham once pointed out the trouble with all these heavens is that they were designed by men for men. Women would have done it so much better.

So nightgowns and harps please and not a single division bell. I beg your pardon, St Peter, which door did you say I had to walk through?

Ann Widdecombe MP

Heaven is in itself eschatological reality. It is the advent of the finally and wholly Other. Its own definitiveness stems from the definitiveness of God's irrevocable and indivisible love. Its openness vis-à-vis the total eschaton derives from the open history of Christ's body, and therewith of all creation which is still under construction. Heaven will only be complete when all the members of the Lord's body are gathered in. Such completion on the part of the body of Christ includes the 'resurrection of the flesh.' It is called the 'Parousia' inasmuch as then the presence of Christ, so far only inaugurated among us, will reach its fullness and encompass all those who are to be saved and the whole cosmos with them.

And so heaven comes in two historical stages. The Lord's exaltation gives rise to the new unity of God with man, and hence to heaven. The perfecting of the Lord's body in the *pleroma* of the 'whole Christ' brings heaven to its true cosmic completion. The individual's salvation is whole and entire only when the salvation of the cosmos and all the elect has come to full fruition. For the redeemed are not simply adjacent to each other in heaven. Rather, in their being together as the one Christ, they *are* heaven. In that moment, the whole creation will become song. It will be a single act in which, forgetful of self, the individual will break through the limits of being into the whole, and the whole take up its dwelling in the individual. It will be joy in which all questioning is resolved and satisfied.

Cardinal Joseph Ratzinger, *Eschatology: Death and Eternal Life*
Prefect of The Sacred Congregaton for the Doctrine of the Faith

This life is a period of training, a time of preparation, during which we learn the art of loving God and our neighbour, the heart of the Gospel message, sometimes succeeding, sometimes failing.

Death is the way which leads us to the vision of God, the moment when we shall see Him as He really is, and find our total fulfilment in love's final choice.

The ultimate union with that which is most lovable, union with God, is the moment of ecstasy, the unending 'now' of complete happiness. That vision will draw from us the response of surprise, wonder and joy which will be forever our prayer of praise. We are made for that.

Cardinal George Basil Hume, OSB, *To Be A Pilgrim*

Are you easy, John, beneath the shining towers?
Do you stand, uncertain, by the pearly gate?
Does the light of glory shine beyond the walls
     Where you wait?

There's a hum of voices round the sapphire throne,
And the sound of footsteps on the streets of gold
As your joyful friends reach out to draw you in
     To the fold.

Lady Mary Wilson
This hitherto unpublished poem is in remembrance
of her friend Sir John Betjeman

Blessed are the poor in spirit,
  for theirs is the kingdom of heaven.
Blessed are those who mourn,
  for they shall be comforted.
Blessed are the meek,
  for they shall inherit the earth.
Blessed are those who hunger and thirst for righteousness,
  for they shall be satisfied.
Blessed are the merciful,
  for they shall obtain mercy.
Blessed are the pure in heart
  for they shall see God.
Blessed are the peacemakers,
  for they shall be called sons of God.
Blessed are those who are persecuted for righteousness' sake,
  for theirs is the kingdom of heaven.
Blessed are you when men revile you and persecute you
  and utter all kinds of evil against you falsely on my account.
Rejoice and be glad,
  for your reward is great in heaven.

Jesus Christ

Index

Index